Pick, Cook and Brew

By the same author (published by Sphere Books Ltd.):

HERBS FOR HEALTH AND BEAUTY
HOME WINE MAKING AND BREWING
CONVERTING A COTTAGE

Pick, Cook and Brew

SUZANNE BEEDELL

PELHAM BOOKS

First published in Great Britain by PELHAM BOOKS LTD
52 Bedford Square, London, W.C.1
1973

ISBN 7207 0634 3

Set and printed in Great Britain by
Tonbridge Printers Ltd, Peach Hall Works, Tonbridge, Kent
in Garamond eleven on twelve point on paper supplied by
P. F. Bingham Ltd, and bound by Dorstel Press,
Harlow

To my mother, who remembers our
blackberry days

Author's Note

Detailed drawings and descriptions are given for identification. Make sure that the herbs you gather for use are, in fact, the ones described in this book.

Contents

Illustrations

107 line drawings of plants, in text.

Acknowledgements

Picking flowers and fruit and cooking them is one thing, typing out recipes is another, and my thanks are due to Ginette Leach who did 75 per cent of the typing, and a great deal of work collecting and checking recipes. Thanks also to those who have passed recipes on to me, and to those who have fearlessly eaten and drunk some of our concoctions, without, I am glad to say, any ill effects at all! Thanks also to my husband Harry and daughter Catherine, who sometimes have to wait a long time for meals to appear on the table while I am busy writing about cooking.

Picture Credits

Figures nos. 3, 12, 27, 33, 48, 65, 66, 78, 79, 83, 84 and 105 have been specially drawn for this book by Dennis Harle. The remainder are taken from *Illustrations of The British Flora* (L. Reeve & Co. Ltd.), which were drawn by the nineteenth-century artist W. H. Fitch, F.L.S., by W. G. Smith, F.L.S., and others.

Introduction

'Better is a dinner of herbs where love is, than a stalled ox and hatred therewith.'   Proverbs xv, 17.

When I was a child, it was always a great day when my mother said 'Let's go blackberrying.' We had our favourite blackberry field, a couple of sandy, rabbit-infested acres beside a wood, dotted all over with big bramble bushes. I never knew who it belonged to, and there was never so much as an old donkey grazing there, though the grass was always short. Perhaps the rabbits kept it down. The blackberries were marvellous, still in my memory the biggest, most succulent, and perfect fruit I have ever seen. I didn't mind the scratches on my arms and legs, and with several of us picking, we would soon get the twenty pounds or so my mother needed for jam. I never ate very many, for I didn't like the rather gritty texture of the fruit; but my purple stained hands and fingers tasted good when I sucked them to clean off the juice. We would stagger home, with the juice making the paper linings of the baskets soggy, and after a day when the house smelt richly of boiling fruit and sugar, there would be rows of gleaming jars full of purple jam, all labelled carefully, ready to put away on the shelves with the marmalade, the plum, the gooseberry jam and all the rest. My mother used to make pounds and pounds of jam, and I suppose we ate it all sooner or later. We were but a small family, and looking back it seems that we must have got through several pounds a week to clear the shelves before the next picking season. I think my mother enjoyed the picking and the jam making for their own sakes, just as much as I did, and probably gave away a lot of it. There was also the enormous satisfaction of getting something almost for nothing; and the end product did taste infinitely better than the stuff we bought at the grocer's.

Yet, although my mother was a countrywoman born, she never cooked any other berries which grew wild. Everything else, I was told, was 'deadly poison'. I suppose she was right to be very firm in her warnings, for so many bright berries which children might be tempted to pick and eat are poisonous: jacks in the pulpit, deadly nightshade, yew, wild bryony in particular; but harmless elderberries were also left alone, and sloes and crab apples were only there to play practical jokes with. Our town cousins got tricked into biting those mouth-shrinking 'wild plums' and 'wild apples'.

I learned to identify mushrooms early on in life, and we picked those whenever we could find them. For me they were just an excuse for early morning bicycle rides in the dew-soaked autumn countryside. We gathered sacks of the sweet chestnuts which grew in the woods. But there it ended, and even when I grew up and was a farmer myself, I never bothered with all those other 'weeds' which I now know to be edible, which were there for the picking.

Only through a growing interest in cooking did I eventually learn just what there is to be picked, cooked, eaten and enjoyed if you only know what to look for.

Primitive tribes, and there are still many, lived and survived on wild things; not only on animals, fish and insects, but also on fruits, roots and leaves which grew naturally around them. There are many places in the world where 'civilised' man dies when the native would survive, because he just does not know what is edible and what is not. As tribal cultures developed, the seeds of the wild plants were cultivated, and gradually there evolved the agricultural systems of the world. Plants spread, carried by birds and animals, carried accidentally by man as he travelled about, often across continents and oceans, and carried deliberately by man as he colonised the earth. Plants adapted themselves wherever they could grow in the different climatic zones, while man developed his agriculture until now he has almost forgotten that once all the fruits and vegetables were wild. Unless something grows in his own garden or fields or can be bought in a shop, he is not very interested in it – it seems to him something neither so good, so tasty, nor desirable.

Man has also forgotten that most ancient medicine was herbal, and that our ancestors ate a lot of things because they knew them to be medicinal, not only nice to taste. Nowadays, for instance, most of us eat garlic and dill for their flavours, not because they are health-giving and digestive. There is no reason why one should not enjoy food for both reasons, as we still do apples and citrus fruit.

But every action has a reaction, and some of us are reacting to the pollution of our world, to the synthetisation of our food supplies, to the ever-increasing flood of frozen, dried, canned and instant food which fills our shops; by seeking at least a part of our food supply in its natural form, not grown in an atmosphere of pesticides and selective weedkillers, not over-stimulated by chemical fertilisers; although it is hard indeed to find plants, even in the wildest places, untouched by drifts of chemical spray, or atmospheric pollution from factory or motor car. Perhaps the most persuasive arguments of all are that wild plants provide foods which do you good, taste good, and are there for the picking.

One word of warning here. When I was farming, I did not like people raiding my property and going off with the mush-rooms which I had been saving for myself, or to sell, but pro-vided they didn't leave gates open, break down my hedges and fences, bring dogs on to the place or allow children to worry the stock, I did not mind blackberry pickers. Wild places, woods, sand dunes, heaths and mountains are generally open to the public; but don't go on to farms, or into carefully fenced areas without first asking permission. The reasons for fences may not be apparent to you, but they are often for game preservation and protection, and in any case, there are strict laws of trespass.

Very few of the plants mentioned in this book are rarities, but whatever the plant is, it should never be totally denuded, destroyed, broken or uprooted. Take no more than you need, and think first of protecting and preserving the countryside, not destroying it. There is a natural law by which, if the numbers of any species drop below a certain point, there are not enough left for that species to perpetuate itself. Nature takes her own tremendous toll and the percentage of survival of all species in relation to the numbers of seeds it produces is tiny. Even though a species seems plentiful to you, it may be in danger, if only locally, if hit too hard. The American passerine pigeon, which was present in so many hundreds of thousands that it was a devastating pest, was killed off in the States to the point where it could not survive as a species, and became, eventually from natural causes, totally extinct. Exactly the same thing can happen to plants, and what may have been a well established species may totally disappear from one area for good if overpicked. This has happened to wild orchids, once far more common than they are now.

Near my home in north Norfolk, primroses grew in profusion in the fenced part of the woods, but never outside the fences, only because generations of children picked them where they could get at them. Primroses and cowslips take years to re-establish themselves if over-picked, or if the roots are dug up, and in this particular instance they have become locally completely extinct.

CHAPTER ONE

The Harvest

All the plants mentioned in this book grow wild somewhere in the United Kingdom. Some are widespread, some are local. Some grow in the north and not in the south, some grow only on chalk or limestone, others only on sand or near the sea; some in woods, some in damp places, some on the seashore. Some of the plants have grown here from time immemorial, others have been brought here deliberately or accidentally by people from other countries, some by birds and animals. Others have escaped from gardens, perhaps centuries ago, others only recently. All have colonised, and have adapted themselves to grow wild under varying soils and climatic conditions, and no longer need the hand of man to cultivate and propagate them.

THE PLANTS

Most of the British wild plants mentioned in this book also grow wild in the parts of the United States that have a temporate climate, or are cultivated in gardens. Some are widespread, others are local; some grow only in woods, in damp places, or by the seashore. Some have grown in North America from time immemorial, others have been brought in deliberately or accidentally from the Old World. Others have escaped from cultivation to grow wild.

The common names of many identical plants differ throughout the world. Basswood, for instance, is lime in Britain, and linden in Europe. In all three places its Latin name is Tilia. Therefore if American readers have any doubts as to the

17

identity of a plant, they should look it up in an American Flora, and cross check the Latin name given there with the Latin name in this book.

There are many other fruits and plants growing wild in the United States, and some species closely related to British ones, but slightly different, which are good to cook and eat. Although these may not be specifically mentioned here, provided that you know them to be harmless, cook them according to the recipes given for similar fruits and plants.

HARVESTING WILD BERRIES, FLOWERS, LEAVES, NUTS, ETC.
Unless it is to be dried or otherwise preserved, the crop should always be cooked or eaten as soon as possible. As soon as anything is picked it begins the processes of decay; fruit has natural yeasts on it which cause it to ferment, and moulds grow very quickly. Leaves and blossoms, especially if compressed and if air is excluded from them, either go mouldy, or begin to decompose and heat. Plunge your hand into a bag of elder-flowers an hour after they have been picked and you will feel the warmth of the beginning of this process. Therefore one should never pick more of anything than can be used up almost immediately. Polythene bags are marvellous for harvesting because juices and moisture do not come through them or soften them, but unless you are taking the crop straight home, empty it into an open polythene bucket so that the air can get to it. Don't use metal collecting containers, as some juices react with the metal to cause staining or colour or taste changes. It is always best to use wooden spoons and plastic, ceramic or enamel containers when making wine or herbal mixtures, although aluminium saucepans are commonly used for cooking vegetables and fruit for immediate consumption.

When collecting nuts, always de-husk them – remove any green outer cases or twigs and leaves of walnuts, chestnuts and cob nuts.

When picking blossoms, take only a proportion of those on the tree or bush, always leave some to grow on and make fruit and seed. Take blossoms carefully without crushing them, and leave behind as much leaf and stalk as possible. Try not to bruise fruit, flowers or leaves, as this hastens decomposition. Leaves should be picked carefully and laid in a box or basket, not stuffed any old how into a bag. Dig up roots and brush off surplus earth on the spot. Don't cut into roots with the spade, and never take more than you need.

It is important to pick all wild plants when they are at their best to get fullest flavour and goodness from them. Flowers should be picked when they are full out, in sunshine, dry and unfaded, preferably in the morning. Pick neither flower buds, nor faded blooms, and don't pick under dull skies and rain. Nectar flows in flowers when the sun is out and it is then that they are fullest of flavour and goodness. Bees, butterflies and other insects will tell you when flowers are ready to pick. They only go to flowers when nectar is flowing.

Fruit should be fully ripe, never under-ripe with some parts still green, and never over-ripe with parts of the fruit mushy or mouldy.

Leaves are best picked in spring, when they are young and full of growth and sap. Old autumnal leaves have little goodness or flavour left in them. Roots are at their best in autumn, when the plant tops are dying back for the winter. The roots have spent all summer storing food to carry the plant through to the following spring.

Herbs for drying should be gathered just before they flower.

Never go picking with bare legs; nettles and brambles are everywhere and can cause havoc. Failing trousers and socks and shoes or wellingtons, sheets of newspaper wrapped round the legs and tied on with string make jolly good nettle shields. When you have finished picking, don't leave the sheets of paper to blow around the countryside! Sometimes thin gloves are useful, and a tube of anti-sting cream can save a lot of moaning and groaning from the younger members of the picking party. A picking stick is a very useful tool. Make one by inserting a piece of stiff wire, or the top of a wire coat hanger into the top of a bamboo cane, or lashing it firmly to one end. Use it to pull thin branches of blackberry bushes, etc., down to hand without breaking them. Don't let children eat too much fruit as they pick it, or badly upset tummies can result.

Never pick alongside main roads, as dirt from the road, dust, pollution from exhaust fumes, will be all over the plants, and nowadays verges are often sprayed with 'selective' weed-killers. Even around fields, watch out for weedkillers. Crops

which have no weeds or flowers growing in them have probably been sprayed, and some of the spray will undoubtedly
have blown on to the hedgerows. If any part of a field bank
or hedge is going brown, or if the leaves of some plants are
twisted and distorted, it is a certain sign of spraying.

When picking mushrooms, use a sharp knife and cut them
from the lower part of the stems, brush off any dirt before
putting the fungus into the bag, then they will not need much
cleaning before being cooked and eaten.

DRYING HERBS

In many cases dried herbs are easier to use than fresh herbs,
and it is always nice to have a supply in the winter. Unfortunately temperatures and humidity are not suitable in this country
for proper out-door herb drying, except during heat waves,
when herbs can be dried hung in loose bunches under trees or
spread out on trays or racks, in the shade. Never dry herbs in
continual direct sunlight, as this evaporates off a lot of the
qualities.

Kitchens and bathrooms are always humid, and so are greenhouses if there is any soil in them, and airing cupboards if
they contain clothes. Empty airing cupboards, or greenhouses
without soil make good drying rooms, as does any well-
ventilated shed or garage in which you can put a heater. Even
a south-facing windowsill will do, but will probably be too
sunny. Don't use a heater which gives off fumes.

Lay herbs out on trays or racks made by tacking old net
curtain material or even wire netting over wooden frames.
Old picture frames will serve. The air must be able to circulate,
and it should be possible to shake the rack and to turn the
herbs. Or tie the herbs into small loose bunches and hang them
up. During the first twenty-four hours, the temperature must
be high, up to 90°F. (32°C.) to get rid of the greater part of
the moisture in the herbs. Turn the plants several times. After
the first day, keep the temperature at about 70°F. (21°C.) for
another week, and the herbs should be dry enough to store.
Turn them once a day, and don't add new material which just
brings in more humidity. When properly and fully dry, leaves
and stems become crisp and snap and powder easily; petals
become papery; roots must be brittle right through; seeds

crack and crumble between the fingernails. Pick over the material, and rub it down between the fingers to the desired size. Electric grinders will break seeds right down if required. Put the dried herbs into brown paper bags (never plastic, as it cannot breathe) and put them in a dry place where they cannot re-absorb moisture. Small quantities can be kept in airtight jars, but never in tins. If the containers are not light-proof, keep them in the dark.

STORING NUTS

Spread the nuts out for a while on a shelf or tray to dry out before putting them in sacks in a dry place, not in paper or polythene bags. Nuts may go mouldy if they have been gathered fresh, if the moisture given off as they dry out is trapped in a container. Check over and shake up bags of nuts every week or two; pick out the mouldy ones, and make sure that the rest are drying well.

DEEP FREEZING

Blanch herbs in boiling water for about a minute. Drain them and put them in small waxed cardboard containers. Seal them and put them into the freezer immediately.

Methods of deep freezing wild fruit, etc., are exactly the same as for cultivated fruits, and the instructions given in any deep freeze manual or recipe book can be safely followed.

CHAPTER TWO

Using the Harvest

Throughout this book there are recipes for cooking fruit and vegetables in many ways. In order to save repetition, and to help if you wish to cook or preserve something for which there is no recipe in the book, I give in this chapter some of the most frequently used basic methods. There are always slight variations, but as all cooking is a matter of variations on basic themes, there is no need to be at a loss just because you cannot find a specific recipe, and there is so much room for experimentation. We all know the traditional combinations, like lamb and mint sauce, beef and horseradish; but the cook who wants to make a name for herself can try out new combinations, many of which are suggested in this book, and some she can discover for herself.

Undoubtedly many dishes are improved by being cooked in wine, yet in this country, where wine is so expensive, we have never really developed a national style of wine cookery. Home-made wines from country fruits are so cheap that one can afford to slosh them around much more freely, and although I always keep the best bottles and the best brews for drinking, there is often the odd bottle which has not cleared or is a little too sweet or dry, or which just does not taste quite right, which will vastly improve some cooked dish. When I make a stew or a pot roast or any meat or poultry dish in a casserole or fireproof dish, I always use home-made wine instead of water to moisten the meat; and this adds flavour to the meat and quality to the gravy.

Always use good ingredients to get good results. Butter,

olive oil, or best cooking oil for frying, home-made wine, liqueurs, brandy, sherry, etc. All these things may seem expensive and extravagant, but so little is needed that the extra cost is not enormous, and the final results are just that much better. So, if you want a reputation as a splendid cook, use good ingredients.

HERB TEAS

Almost all the herbs mentioned in this book can be used, singly or in combinations, to make herbal teas, often with considerable medicinal and cosmetic uses, a subject covered in an earlier book by the author.*

Many people drink herb teas just for their taste and refreshing qualities, and in Britain we are rather stuck on 'tea', usually Indian, and outside health food shops and herbalist shops, it is almost impossible to buy made-up herbal teas. Yet in other countries many different kinds of herbal teas are drunk regularly and in preference to 'tea' as we know it. A recent international expedition to Mount Everest took among its supplies, quantities of different herbal teas to cater for the tastes of its members.

Throughout this book, unless it is specifically stated otherwise, use the following method to make herbal teas:

Take a china or glass teapot and warm it just as you would for ordinary tea. A glass teapot is rather fun because you can see the unusual and delicate colours of some of the teas. Put the herbs into the pot and pour on boiling water just as when making ordinary Indian tea. Allow the tea to brew in the pot for 5 minutes before pouring it out.

Quantities: When using fresh herbs, use 3 teaspoonsful of the herb for each cup, plus 3 for the pot. Crush or bruise the herb inside a clean dry cloth before putting it in the pot. This means that to make any quantity of tea, you will need quite a big pot. What is left can be strained off and kept in the fridge to be drunk iced, but it should be used up within a couple of days or it may ferment. (It is fermenting when bubbles start rising.)

When using dried herbs, use 1 teaspoonful of herbs for

Herbs for Health and Beauty S. M. Beedell, Sphere Books Ltd.

each cup and one for the pot, just as for ordinary tea.

To make tea from aromatic seeds, bruise the seeds and put 1 teaspoonful per pint into boiling water in an enamel saucepan, simmer for 5 minutes, strain and serve hot.

To avoid using a strainer, herbs can be put into muslin bags and used just like teabags, but it is rather a lot of trouble to go to.

Sweeten the tea with sugar or honey to taste, and even add milk to it if you like it that way, although herb tea is usually drunk 'straight'. Some teas are improved by adding a slice of lemon. Add herbs to ordinary China tea, to achieve a 'different' flavour.

Do remember that some herbs may have quite strong medicinal effects, and should not be drunk in enormous quantities. The usual dose for medicinal herbs is 3 wineglassfuls per day; the equivalent of not more than 2 teacups, so take note of the possible medicinal effects, where stated, before drinking too much!

HERB LIQUEURS

Liqueurs are very easy to make but not particularly cheap, as the base has to be brandy or gin or some other expensive spirit. However, as sugar or honey is always added, and juices from berries, you should end up with more liquid than you started with, and the cost, per bottle, is considerably less than that of bought liqueurs. The tastes are marvellous. Many people are a bit afraid to use expensive spirit in case something goes wrong, and the whole lot has to be thrown out, but actually nothing can go wrong. Alcohol inhibits fermentation, and there is already so much alcohol in the spirit that fermentation cannot restart. All that happens is that the alcohol dissolves out the flavours and colours of the herbs or fruit which have been added, and the sugar or honey sweetens the drink and counteracts any sourness from the fruit.

Most proprietory liqueurs are made from fruit and/or herbs steeped in spirit, sugar and honey, and the recipes are carefully guarded secrets; so it is only by experimentation that you may produce something that tastes exactly like Benedictine or Drambuie. But liqueurs such as Cherry Brandy are extremely easy to reproduce, and the most famous country liqueur of all,

Sloe Gin, is as good as any liqueur ever made and ridiculously easy to make.

Detailed recipes are given under the different herb headings, but all the equipment you need is one large screw-topped jar or Kilner jar which does not leak when turned upside down. To each jar half full of berries, add $\frac{1}{2}$ lb. of sugar or honey and top up with spirit. Screw the jar down tightly, and turn it upside down once a week for three months, or longer if you can wait. Strain off the liquid, bottle it, and don't drink it too quickly!

To make herb liqueurs, add spirit to the $\frac{1}{2}$ lb. sugar and put in the herbs, tied in a muslin bag. Steep them for three months or longer until the liqueur has acquired flavour, and bottle as above.

To make strong syrup for ratafias, liqueurs, etc., add just enough water to the sugar in a saucepan to cover it. Boil it very gently for a long time, removing the scum frequently. The longer the simmering, the stronger the syrup. Bottle it for later use. If you wish it to be exceptionally clear, add well-beaten egg whites to the hot syrup, mix them well, and strain the syrup through a jelly bag.

WINE MAKING

The basic principle of wine making is that when yeast is mixed with sugar, water and organic matter in a closed container, it grows. Fermentation takes place producing an enzyme called zymase which breaks down sugar molecules to obtain oxygen, releasing 48 per cent CO_2 and 47 per cent alcohol from any given quantity of sugar as a byproduct. This alcohol (happily) remains in the water and fermentation will continue until there is so much alcohol present that it inhibits fermentation. It follows that if a minimum amount of sugar (about 2 lb. per gallon of liquid or 'must') is added, the yeast will use it all up before there is enough alcohol to inhibit fermentation, and the wine will be very dry. If more sugar, up to 4 lb. per gallon of must, is added the fermentation will cease when the alcohol content inhibits it, and some sugar will still be left unused, so the wine will be sweet. When alcohol is added to a wine to fortify it, fermentation will slow down or cease, so never do this early on in fermentation.

In order that wine shall have flavour, the must is made by soaking fruits, blossoms, berries, leaves or roots in water.

Citric acid, tannin, and nutrient are also needed to help proper fermentation, and when these things are lacking in the fruit or whatever it is that you are using to flavour the wine, then they must be added. Citric acid can be added by using tartaric acid powder or citric acid crystals, or by using lemon juice. Eight lemons produce as much juice as 1 oz. of citric acid crystals. Actually one rarely needs to add more than ½ oz., and many fruits are already so acid, that no addition is needed at all. Tannin is present in sufficient quantities in most fruits, but if necessary it can be added as tannin powder, or cold tea. I always add a couple of tablespoons of cold tea to my wines, even if it is not strictly necessary.

Nutrient salts (ammonium phosphate) can be added to the must to make up for organic deficiencies, and they do ensure a good long fermentation. Some winemakers prefer to add raisins to provide extra nutrient for the yeast, but the raisin flavour is so strong that it can dominate the delicate tastes of some wines and spoil them.

Yeast can be bought from winemaker's suppliers in different 'types' – all-purpose, Burgundy, Champagne, etc., but for all but very advanced winemakers, I think that general-purpose yeast, or even ordinary baker's dried yeast, is perfectly satisfactory. Until one has mastered the art of producing fairly consistent wines, there is not much point in using special yeasts. Some natural or wild yeasts are present on fruit, flowers, etc., (must from grapes does not have yeast added to it, as the right natural yeasts are present), but it is safer not to rely on these for fermentation as they may be the wrong yeasts and just make the wine 'go bad'. Campden tablets (sulphur dioxide) are commonly used to sterilise the must and destroy wild yeasts, but if used in too great a quantity, will slow down or prevent fermentation in the added yeast. I usually add one Campden tablet to each gallon of must as I make it, never more than two, although some winemakers believe that one tablet is not enough.

Making the Must
Whichever method is used, the aim is to extract the flavour

from the main ingredients, to add dissolved sugar and necessary acids, nutrients, etc., and to start fermentation with added yeast. There is no one method which is better than any other, and the winemaker will, by experience, find the one which works best for him. Because a recipe gives specific instructions to use one method, it does not necessarily mean that the same ingredients cannot be combined by other methods.

Method 1. Put the fruit, flowers, and other organic ingredients into a clean polythene bucket or dustbin (cleanliness of all equipment is absolutely vital), and pour boiling water over them, using about ⅔ of the total quantity of water. Cover and leave for 2 days, stirring occasionally. Then strain the juice and pour it into fermentation jars, leaving them ⅔ full. Using the other ⅓ of water, make a syrup by dissolving the sugar in it in a saucepan, and top up the bottles with this, leaving room for the addition of citrus juice, tannin, cold tea, nutrients, or whatever, leaving about 2 in. space clear below the cork. The yeast, mixed at least 2 hours before with a little of the must and sugar, should be added when the must has cooled to a temperature of 70°F. (21°C.) or thereabouts (it feels only barely warm to the touch). For a day or two the fermentation will be fierce and the jar may be lightly stoppered with a plug of cotton wool. When the fermentation dies down sufficiently, top up to within ½ in. of the cork, which is inserted with a fermentation lock in it.

Method 2. The same, but use the full amount of water, and make a syrup by dissolving the sugar into the strained must, bringing it to just below boiling point in a saucepan. The disadvantage of this method is that some flavour may go off in the steam if the liquid is allowed to boil.

Method 3. All the ingredients are put into the bucket with the boiling water, and when it has cooled the yeast is added and the first few days' fermentation is allowed to take place in the bucket. Wine must ferment anaerobically (without air) and as long as it is in the bucket it is fermenting as beer does, aerobically; in the presence of air, which if it goes on too long will affect the flavour. So the liquid must be strained into fermentation jars within 4 or 5 days.

By the same token, the liquid in the bottles must be topped up just below the cork, or as it ferments it will also oxydise

and the finished wine will have a characteristic and indescrib-
ably nasty smell and taste. This taste is so often the pre-
dominant one of wines made by beginners who do not realise
that it is necessary to exclude air from all processes as much
as possible once fermentation has begun. Imperfectly corked
wine may also acquire this flavour as air gets into the bottle,
and will often grow a crust of mould from airborne spores.

A fermentation lock which allows gas to escape without
any air getting in is then inserted and the wine left in a
fairly warm place (about 65°F. or 18°C.) but out of direct
sunlight, to ferment to a finish.

The yeast throws a sediment which sinks to the bottom with
particles of matter floating in the wine. When fermentation is
finished no more gas bubbles will be coming through the
lock and the wine will begin to clear.

At this stage rack it off carefully into another jar, using a
piece of rubber or polythene tube as a siphon, or using a
patent siphon from a winemaker's shop, always being careful
not to take too much sediment into the new bottle. Top it
up to just below the cork with a little boiled water, cork it
firmly, and leave it for three months in a cool place. Take it
out and have a look at it, and if it has thrown a lot of
sediment, rack it again. Leave it in its jar until it has cleared
completely and then siphon it carefully into clean bottles and
cork it down.

Pectin is an essential ingredient of wine, which is present
in most fruits. Crushing the fruit and heat sterilisation with
boiling water releases the pectin into the must, (which makes
it cloudy) but kills some of the natural enzymes which later
break down the pectin and clarify the wine. Some winemakers add pectin enzyme to the must before adding the
yeast, to replace that which is destroyed. The addition of a
little pectozyme to racked wine which has not cleared will
often help it clear, but failing this use finings which can be
bought from a winemaking shop, or add a couple of teaspoonsful of beaten egg white to each gallon of wine. Usually
haze will clear without any interference if the wine is left
alone long enough, so don't be in too much of a hurry to mess
about with it if there is any sign of a bright clear layer of
wine in the jar.

If wine is bottled from the maturing jar when it is still fermenting ever so slightly, and the cork is wired down, a sparkling wine will result. Most beginners achieve this by luck rather than judgement. So often a wine is bottled just a little too soon and blows its cork, spilling most of the contents, so don't be in too much of a hurry to bottle the wine. It goes without saying that the longer you can wait before drinking the wine the better it will be. Six months is the absolute minimum, and some wines will be drinkable at that time, but they will be just that much better after a year. If you are making more than one jar of a wine at a time, always try to 'lose' one jar after the last racking, and bottle the rest. Then in a year (or two) find the unbottled jar and bottle its contents and call it a 'special'!!

Bottles are best stored in a rack on their sides. This ensures that the base of the cork is covered with wine, and any sediment will slide down to the bottom corner of the bottle.

Always pick out a bottle several hours before you wish to drink it, and stand it upright. If there is any sediment lying along the bottle, it will usually drop quickly to the bottom and the wine can be decanted leaving it behind. Follow the same rules as for all wine – serve red wines at room temperature or very slightly warmer, and chill white ones.

The following direction give the basics of wine making: *

Equipment needed: 1. Polythene bucket or other lidded container. 2. Nylon or cloth strainer. 3. One-gallon glass fermentation jars. 4. Fermentation lock with cork. 5. Siphon tube. 6. Clean wine bottles and new corks.

A hydrometer with which to measure the specific gravity and thereby sugar and alcohol content of the must, and wine at all stages, is a most useful piece of extra equipment. So is a wooden 'cork flogger'. All these things can be bought at winemaker's suppliers, and come with full instructions as to use.

Do make sure that everything is clean; use polythene, ceramic and glass containers, and wooden spoons.

When using citrus fruits, never allow any of the white pith to get into the wine, or it will make it very bitter.

---

*For very full instructions see: *Home Wine Making and Brewing* by the same author, published by Sphere Books Ltd.

Don't use too much or too many chemicals.

Don't use too many raisins.

Don't leave too big an air space between liquid and corks in jars and bottles.

Don't make wine too sweet. It can only be helped by blending it with very dry wine, whereas dry wine can always be sweetened by adding sugar or honey.

Keep wine in jars at an even temperature, about 65°F. (18°C.)

Make wine as soon as possible after fruit, flowers, etc., have been picked.

Don't use dirty, or mouldy or badly damaged ingredients.

Stick to simple recipes to start with.

All wine recipes in this book require the wine to be fermented to a finish, racked at least once, and left at least three months to mature before being bottled.

FRUIT SYRUPS

Grandma used to make blackcurrant syrup for coughs, and during the last war rose hip syrup became very popular for its high vitamin content; but in this country we have never bothered very much with syrups. Actually they are a most useful addition to the larder and jolly good poured over milk puddings or jellies or ice-cream, or incorporated in other sweet dishes, as well as to drink.

Use over-ripe but not mouldy fruit. Rinse it in cold water without bruising it. Put it in a basin which can be stood in a saucepan of hot water. Add enough water to cover the bottom of the basin. Let it cook gently until it is soft enough to squash with a wooden spoon, not longer than half an hour. The fruit can be cooked directly in a saucepan with a little water, but take great care it does not stick or scorch.

Some fruit needs special treatment, and this is detailed under individual headings.

The juice is then strained through a fine sieve or a jelly bag. If you wish to use the syrup undiluted, add about 4 oz. of white sugar to each pint, depending on the natural sweetness of the fruit. Syrup which is intended to be diluted should have about 1 lb. of sugar to each pint of juice. Stir the sugar into the juice until it is dissolved and then pour the liquid into warmed Kilner jars or bottles. Boil new corks for ½ hour before using them and cork the bottles of syrup, leaving 1½ in. between the top of the syrup and the cork. Tie down the corks by making a loop about an inch long in the centre of a piece of string about 10 in. long. Tie the string tightly round the neck of the bottle, then pass one end through the loop and pull it down across the cork, tying it down tightly again. Stand the bottles or jars in warm water just as one does when preserving fruit, not allowing the bottles to touch the bottom of the pan. The water should come up to the necks, but not over the corks. Heat the lot until it is just simmering and let it go on simmering for ½ hour.

BOTTLING FRUIT

There are three ways of bottling fruit, and each has its uses. If the appearance of the fruit is not important, then the fruit can be stewed and bottled either whole or sieved, although even if unsieved it will be bound to be broken. Add just enough water to stop the fruit from burning, and about a cupful of sugar per lb. of fruit. Bring it to the boil, and let it cook for 5 minutes, and pour it straight into preserving jars which have already been thoroughly heated. Preserving jars must always be hot when hot fruit is put into them, or they may crack. The bottles are usually made of fairly tough glass so that they will stand oven heating, or being stood in boiling water, or having boiling water poured into them, but they should always be warmed first over the stove, to lessen the risk of breakage. Don't forget to heat the bottles' tops and rings as well.

The oven method of bottling is best for most fruit. Clean fruit is packed carefully into the bottles, which are then stood in the oven. Make sure the bottles do not touch each other. Put a lid or piece of baking foil loosely over the top of each jar, so that the fruit does not scorch, and set the oven at 250°F. (121°C.). Leave the fruit in the oven for at least an hour. It should then look cooked right through the jar. Make a water syrup using ½ lb. sugar per pint of water. Take one jar at a time out of the oven and fill it immediately with syrup, making sure that there are no air bubbles among the fruit. Seal the jar immediately.

The third method is to heat the fruit in its syrup in the bottles, in a pan containing water. This method causes less damage to the fruit than the previous methods. Pack the fruit into cold bottles, make a syrup as above, and when it is cold, top up the bottles with it. Put on the lids and immerse the jars in a pan of cold water. Metal lids can be screwed right down, but glass lids with metal rings should not be screwed too tightly, in order to let air escape as it heats and expands. The jars must not stand directly on the bottom of the pan. A fish kettle with a perforated strainer to keep the jars off the bottom is fine for the job, but failing that, make a trellis of pieces of wood on which to stand the jars. The jars should not touch each other. Cover the pan and heat the whole lot gradually until the water is simmering gently. This should take about an hour. Allow it to simmer for about 20 minutes. Remove the bottles, first dipping out some of the water so that you can grasp them with a cloth, and tighten the screw bands.

A properly sealed jar, whatever the bottling method, can be safely picked up by the lid without it coming off, even after the screw bands and metal clips have been removed. Test jars this way to make sure they have sealed properly. If they have not, reheat them and try again. Otherwise after a while the contents may go mouldy.

JAM MAKING

Jam is made by boiling fruit in a little water until it is soft, then adding enough sugar to preserve it and make it set, and boiling it, stirring regularly, until the right proportion of sugar to fruit and juice is achieved. It is a bit of a hit-or-miss process, and some fruits contain substances which help them to set, so do not need so much sugar. Too much sugar makes very firm, sweet jam, too little sugar makes well-flavoured runny jam which will not keep very long. A setting agent (pectin) can be added and this helps to make the better-flavoured jams using less sugar, or with fruit that does not contain natural pectin. Jam will set which consists of about $\frac{2}{3}$ sugar. In other words, 3 lb. of sugar will make about 5 lb. of jam. As a rule of thumb, use 1 lb. sugar per 1 lb. fruit, and let it boil down until it no longer runs off a wooden spoon. Hold up the spoon with which you have been stirring the jam. At first the jam will run off, but it will gradually make longer drips until the last big drip coagulates into a flake. If jam is overboiled it goes dark and treacly. The simplest way of all to tell when jam is ready is to use a cooking thermometer. This most useful piece of equipment is not expensive, and it makes it so easy to be right every time. Jam will set when it has reached a temperature of 220°F. (104°C.).

Once the jam is cooked, leave it to cool a bit, and skim off any scum which has risen to the surface. Use a small jug and pour it into heated jars. Fill the jars to the brim, as jam contracts when it cools and the jars should be as full as possible when sealed to exclude air. Put the little circular tissues which come with jam jar covers on to the jam immediately the jars are filled and smooth them down. This helps to keep out unwanted air. As soon as the jars are cool enough to handle, put the covers on tightly. The sooner jam is covered the better.

JELLY

Fruit jellies are a little more trouble to make than jam, but are delicious and well worth it. Use the same amount of sugar as for jam. Use slightly under-ripe fruit, it sets better. Some fruits do not set well and are best combined with others which are good setters. Apple is full of pectin and is used in lots of combinations with other fruit both in jams and jellies. Gooseberries, blackcurrants, damsons, quinces, rowanberries and crab apples are all good setters.

Just put the fruit in enough water to cover it, reducing the amount if the fruit is very juicy. Cook the fruit gently until it is a pulp. Never boil it fast or all the water will evaporate off, and some of the setting qualities of the fruit will be lost. Put the pulp into a jelly bag suspended over a bowl and let it drain, for no longer than 12 hours, or setting quality will be lost. You can squeeze the bag gently to extract the last of the juice, but may risk making the jelly a little cloudy. It is really best left to drip on its own. Some good setting fruits can be reheated in enough water to make a purée, and allowed to drip again. You get to know by experience how well the juice will set by the degree of stickiness it has when it is strained. To make an accurate setting test, put a teaspoonful of the cooked

B

pulp, before straining, into a cup, and set it aside to cool. Then add three teaspoonsful of methylated spirit and shake it up gently. If the pulp is a good setter it will form one lump of jelly. If it is not going to set too well, it will form several clots of jelly, and if it is poor, it will form a lot of small jelly clots. In the latter case, reheat the fruit, and simmer off a little more liquid and test it again. Jelly can be made to set by adding pectin according to the instructions on the bottle, but it is a lot more satisfying to achieve a well-set jelly without resorting to a bottle of pectin!

Once the juice has been strained and tested, add ¾ to 1 lb. of sugar per pint of juice. Put the juice back into a clean pan and heat it up, and then add the sugar, stirring until it has dissolved. Boil it fast for 10 minutes and then check to see if it will set. Use a thermometer as described on page 33 to be absolutely certain. Once again, experience will enable you to use the spoon method. A little jelly put on a cold plate will set after a few moments if it is ready.

Before jelly is bottled it must be carefully skimmed if it is to look brilliant and clear. Do this as soon as it has been taken off the stove. Use a hot clean metal spoon.

Use small jars, not bigger than 1 lb. size. When I was a child, my grandmother always used to make me special personal jars of bramble jelly in fish paste pots, but any small glass or china pots will do. Warm the jars and pour the jelly in just as one pours beer, down the side of the glass. This way fewer air bubbles get caught up to spoil the look of the jelly. Fill the jars right up and put on the waxed paper discs at once. Put on the top covers as soon as the jars are cool enough to handle. Store the jelly in a dark cupboard if possible.

SALADS

Use wild plants in salads in exactly the same way as garden plants. Wash the leaves carefully and serve them crisp and fresh with any kind of dressing you like. Seeds can be sprinkled over salad to give it flavour.

VEGETABLES

The leaves of wild plants are usually cooked in the same way as spinach, or just as one could cook their garden counterparts. They should be carefully washed and put in a saucepan with just enough water to stop them burning, a dash of salt and usually a knob of butter. Put the saucepan over a medium heat and shake it occasionally to prevent sticking and burning, and be sure the contents do not boil dry. Don't overcook any vegetable. If the lid is kept on while cooking moisture is retained and there is less danger of burning, but some cooks claim that the vegetables keep a better colour if cooked without a lid. Drain the vegetables well before serving, add more butter and salt and pepper to taste.

SOUPS
The methods of making soup with wild plants are of course in principle no different when using the ingredients in this book from those used for ordinary cooking; but it may be useful to have them set out here.

All liquid in which vegetables have been boiled should be used for soup, but remember that you have probably salted the water, so don't put more salt in without checking it by taste. Soups can be made from any vegetable; leaf, root, blossom or berry, just by boiling the basic plant with other suggested ingredients, and putting the whole lot through a sieve or blender. This makes a vegetable purée which can be eaten thick or thin, diluted with water, milk, cream, or meat stock, and flavoured to taste. Another method, when less of the vegetable is available, is to make a cream soup by the 'roux' method. A tablespoonful of butter is put into a saucepan and melted, and into this is stirred a level tablespoonful of plain (not self-raising) flour. This is allowed to cook for a minute over a low heat, being stirred to prevent browning. Should it brown the soup will be darker in colour. Then liquid, either the vegetable water, or milk or meat or chicken stock, is gradually added to the roux, which thickens immediately. It must be constantly stirred, and you go on adding liquid until the desired consistency is reached. Any pieces of vegetable which are to be included are then added, either as they are, or having been put through a blender; the seasoning is adjusted and the soup served as the recipe directs.

Some vegetables, such as celery, can be chopped small and cooked in butter until golden, and then added to a cream soup made with a roux as above, in which the liquid is either milk or water in which the celery has been boiled.

A spoonful or two of fresh cream added to a blender soup gives it a better colour and smoother texture.

Arrowroot, cornflour, ground rice, or semolina can also be used to thicken soups and a roux made with them in exactly the same way. If these flours are added to a liquid they receive more cooking while being blended with the butter, and are not quite so 'raw' in the finished soup; and it is very much easier to prevent lumps forming if soup is made this way. If things go very wrong and the soup mixture is lumpy, give it a good mix with an egg beater; this will get rid of a lot of them. Dehydrated potato can also be used to thicken soups.

SAUCES AND MAYONNAISE

Several recipes are included in this book, under specific plant headings, and under Chapter 4, 'Mixed Herb Recipes' for sauces, mayonnaise, etc., but some general hints may be useful. Sauces can be made by the roux method described in the last section, milk being used as the liquid, and flavouring added to what is really Béchamel sauce.

Sauces made with flavouring and stock or milk or cream can be thickened by being put into a double saucepan and having beaten egg yolks added. The mixture must be stirred constantly and not allowed to boil or it will curdle.

Mayonnaise is extremely easy to make, and can be altered and flavoured to taste. Put one beaten egg yolk in a narrow bowl or jug, and add a teaspoonful of lemon juice, a teaspoonful of vinegar (preferably wine vinegar) a pinch of salt and a shake of black pepper, half a teaspoonful of castor sugar, and half teaspoonful of mustard (English dry or French to taste). Beat all this together with an egg beater, and then drip in olive oil or good cooking oil, beating all the time. When the mixture begins to thicken, pour the oil in faster and keep beating until you have blended in at least half a cupful of oil. If the mixture refuses to thicken and go creamy, add another egg yolk and beat it again. The seasonings in this mayonnaise can be altered to taste, and additional flavourings, garlic, tarragon, dill, oregano, or any wild herb you may like, can be blended to this base.

CHAPTER THREE

The Recipes, Plant by Plant

'Cookery means the knowledge of Medea and of Circe and of
Helen and of the Queen of Sheba.

It means the knowledge of all herbs and fruits and balms
and spices, and all that is healing and sweet in the fields
and groves, and savour in meats.'

John Ruskin

AGRIMONY Fam. Rosaceae

Agrimonia eupatoria

A very common plant which grows in grassy places. Never
more than 2 ft. high, it has small yellow flowers on tapering
spikes, and the leaves are softly hairy. Sometimes the plant
is slightly brown, toothed, with smaller leaves between the
bigger ones down the stem.

37

AGRIMONY WINE

Good bunch agrimony	6 lb. Demerara sugar
2 gals. water	1 oz. g.p. yeast
3 lemons	½ oz. root ginger
6 oranges	

Bruise the ginger and put it with the agrimony to boil in the water for ¼ hour. Strain this on to the sugar and the sliced lemons and oranges, with the white pith carefully removed.

When this is cool, add the yeast. Cover it and leave it to stand for 2 days. Strain the liquid into fermentation jars, ferment to a finish, and mature, rack, and bottle.
See also: Wine Making (page 25).

ALEXANDERS Fam. Umbelliferae

Smyrnium olusatrum
Black Lovage

A big bushy plant, growing up to 4 ft. high. It is the only native umbellifer which has big green trifoliate leaves and yellow flowers. The fruits are round and black. It is very common in England on wasteland and cliffs near the sea. It smells a little like celery and its culinary uses are the same, as it was once widely used as a vegetable and for flavouring, until it was displaced by celery.
See also: Celery.

ANGELICA Fam. Umbelliferae

Archangelica officinalis or
Angelica archangelica

This plant, which is found in Britain growing near rivers and in damp places, is an escape, and is related to our native wild angelica (*Angelica sylvestris*). It is a biennial but will re-seed so that it becomes almost perennial. It can grow as tall as 8 ft. and is really a most impressive plant. It is unmistakable because of its size. It has deeply indented and very big leaves, thick, light green hollow stems, and whitish-green flowers like white umbrellas. The stems are hollow and grooved, and it is these stems which have always been used candied to make those attractive and tasty bright green bits for decorating cakes.

Angelica tastes a little like juniper and it is used with juniper to flavour gin. Angelica tea tastes rather like China tea.

The plant grows so big that it gets very woody as the summer goes on, so the flower and leaf stalks for candying should be picked in April or May, otherwise they get much too tough and lose flavour. The leaves, from which tea is made, should also be cut before the middle of June, and dried for all-year-round use. Continual cutting from early in the year will encourage the plant to put out new shoots and leaves, which can be harvested later in the season, but the first growth must be taken early if it is to be used at all. Angelica tea can also be made from the roots of first-year plants, dug in early autumn.

The young shoots of the plant are sometimes used to flavour jam or marmalade, and when blanched can be eaten in salads.

The French and Spanish eat candied angelica as a sweet.

If you add an angelica root or a few pieces of stem to stewing rhubarb, it will offset some of the tartness, so that less sugar need be added; it is useful for diabetics and slimmers.

CANDIED ANGELICA

Green shoots, leaf and flower stalks of angelica	Brine ($\frac{1}{4}$ oz. salt to 4 pts. water) Sugar

This recipe takes about a week to make, so be sure you are going to be around that long before you start! You will also need a cooking thermometer.

Pick the green shoots, and leaf and flower stalks in April or May. Put them to soak in brine for 10 minutes. This keeps them green.

Cook the angelica in enough water to cover it, for 5 to 7 minutes. Drain and scrape it to remove the outer skin. Use the same water to make a syrup of 6 oz. sugar to each $\frac{1}{2}$ pint juice. Put the angelica into a bowl, pour the syrup over it and leave it for 24 hours. Drain off the syrup and add another 2 oz. sugar to every $\frac{1}{2}$ pt. of liquid, and heat it to 225°F. (107°C.) Pour it back into the bowl over the angelica and repeat this process from 3 to 5 times until the juice is the consistency of runny honey. Then reheat the syrup to 245°F. (118°C.), add the angelica and bring it to the boil. Remove it from the heat and allow it to cool, and boil it again. Do this 4 times in all. Leave the whole lot to stand for 2 days. Then drain the angelica and lay it on a rack or mesh. Sprinkle it with sugar and stand it overnight in a very cool oven, set at its lowest rating, until it is dry enough to store in screw top jars.

Use up any spare syrup to sweeten tart stewed fruit such as rhubarb.

ANGELICA LIQUEUR

2 lb. angelica stalks	$\frac{1}{4}$ oz. cinnamon
1 lb. sugar	1 clove
1 qt. brandy	$\frac{1}{4}$ tspn. nutmeg
little water	

Put the angelica stalks, cut in small pieces, into the brandy in a Kilner jar. To make a spicy liqueur add the 3 spices at this stage. Seal the jar well and leave it in a sunny place for about a month.

Dissolve the sugar in a little water and add it to the brandy. Strain the whole lot through a very fine sieve, pressing it well. Leave it to stand for a few hours. If there are any signs of cloudiness in the liqueur, use a filter paper in a funnel when bottling it.

See also: Vespetro (page 208); and Mixed Herb and Spice Liqueur (page 209).

ARCHANGEL Fam. Labiatae

Lamium album
White Dead-nettle

Galeobdolon luteum
Yellow Dead-nettle

White dead-nettle is a hairy, faintly aromatic plant which grows everywhere in England and is a little less common in Ireland and Scotland. It looks a bit like a stinging nettle, but has big white flowers. The yellow dead-nettle is less hairy, with narrower darker leaves, and grows in open woodlands; rare in southern Scotland and south-east Ireland. Henbit has deeply toothed leaves which are much more rounded than those of the two previous plants. It has rich purple flowers, and is common on waste ground that has once been cultivated. The

Lamium amplexicaule   *Lamium purpureum*
Henbit   Red Dead-nettle

red dead-nettle sprawls more than the others, has square stems, leafless below the pinkish purple flowers. The leaves are all stalked and have pointed tips and heart-shaped bases. A very common weed on cultivated ground. When the plant is crushed, it has a pungent smell.

BUTTERED ARCHANGEL TIPS

Young, tender, flowering Salt and pepper
 tips of archangel   Water
Butter

Pick young, tender, flowering tips of dead-nettle and wash them well. Put the damp leaves in a pan with a big knob of butter. Cook them gently until they are tender, turning them occasionally. Season with salt and pepper. Strain them when done, and serve them with more butter. Chopped chives or spring onions can be sprinkled on top.

Ash Fam. Oleaceae

Fraxinus excelsior

The shoots and seeds or 'keys' of the ordinary ash tree can be eaten in salads.

ASH KEY PICKLE

Ash keys	Salt
Water	Spiced vinegar

Boil the keys in 3 successive lots of water until they are tender. Put them in a jar and cover them with salted, spiced vinegar.

Asparagus Fam. Liliaceae

Asparagus grows wild very locally in England, usually in sand dunes or sandy meadows near the sea. Where it does grow it is abundant. It looks exactly the same as the cultivated variety which is always so expensive to buy, and it tastes even better. As the shoots appear in May and June deep among grass, they are hard to find, being green with slightly purplish tinges. The plants grow fast and soon reach up to 4 ft. tall, with feathery, waving fern tops. Use these tops to make tea. The first thick shoots are cooked just as is cultivated asparagus, except that they are much more tender and every bit of the stalk can be eaten. Use the thinner shoots which are turning into fern to make soup or for flavouring. Always keep the water in which asparagus has been cooked to use as a basis for soup.

Asparagus officinalis

All the preparation that is necessary before cooking it, is to trim off any dirty bottoms of the stalks and to wash the vegetable in clean water.

Although there are many recipes for cooking asparagus, perhaps it is never better than just boiled in salted water for about 10 minutes, till it is tender but not mushy, and served immediately with melted butter poured over it. I rate as one of the finest meals I have eaten; fresh picked asparagus, cooked on a picnic stove, on the beach, washed down with home made wine and followed by fresh brown bread and butter and Camembert cheese. The sun was shining, the larks singing, and expensive restaurants with your actual Cordon Bleu cookery seemed totally superfluous!

All kinds of sauces go with asparagus. Put the boiled vegetable into a fireproof dish and cover the stalks with a piece of paper or baking foil, so that the sauce does not get on to them to stick to the eater's fingers. Mornay sauce, sprinkled with Parmesan cheese; Noisette butter, heated with lemon juice in it; cheese sauce or curry sauce. Perhaps finest of all try cold asparagus with home made mayonnaise (see page 36) poured over the tips just before serving.

Asparagus itself makes a good garnish or sauce. Rub tips and tender pieces through a sieve, heat the purée and add butter and cream. Beat the mixture well, but do not make it too thin.

CREAM OF ASPARAGUS SOUP

1 pt. water in which the asparagus has been cooked	Salt and pepper
	3 balm leaves
	Cooked asparagus
2 oz. butter	pieces
1 tbsp. plain flour	Cream

Make a roux by melting the butter in a saucepan and adding the flour. Cook this for a few moments then gradually add the asparagus water, stirring all the time. When the desired consistency has been reached, add a little cream. Add the asparagus pieces chopped fairly small, let the whole lot cook gently for a few minutes and season it to taste. Serve this soup either hot or ice cold.

ASPARAGUS PURÉE SOUP

Asparagus water	Butter
Pieces of asparagus	Salt and pepper
Flour	Cream

If you have a lot of asparagus pieces boil them in salted water and put the whole lot through a sieve or blender or liquidiser. Make a roux using half the quantities recommended in the previous recipe, and add the purée gradually to this. Season to taste, and stir in a little cream.

ASPARAGUS COUNTRY SALAD

1 lb. asparagus	Lemon juice
Olive oil	1 tspn. chervil
1 tspn. chopped tarragon	1 cup chopped cooked
2 tspn. shallot	chicken
Curry powder	Home-made mayonnaise
Salted water	2 chopped red chillies

Cook the asparagus in the usual way, drain it and cut it into 1 in. lengths. Season these with olive oil, lemon juice tarragon, chervil and shallot. Arrange the chicken pieces in a border on a flat dish. Cover these with mayonnaise and a dusting of dry curry powder. Garnish the whole lot with small, finely chopped, seed-free red chillies.

ASPARAGUS WITH HARD EGGS

Cooked asparagus	Butter
Hard-boiled eggs	

Boil the asparagus in the normal way and serve it with hard-boiled eggs, cut into halves. The eater mashes up the egg with the melted butter.

ASPARAGUS WITH SOFT EGGS

Cooked asparagus	Butter
Soft-boiled eggs	

Serve soft-boiled eggs with cooked asparagus and melted butter. Dip the asparagus first into the butter then into the egg.

ASPARAGUS WITH FRIED BREAD

Asparagus	Butter
Stale bread	Parmesan cheese

Boil the asparagus tips in salted water for 8 minutes, drain and sauté them in butter until they are tender. Slice some stale bread in pieces about 4 in. long and half as wide, and fry them in more butter. Put about 6 asparagus tips on each slice of bread, sprinkle them with Parmesan cheese, pour some of the butter the tips were cooked in over the lot, and brown them lightly under the grill.

ASPARAGUS FRIED IN BATTER

Asparagus	Lemon juice
Olive oil	Light batter
Water	Salt and pepper

Cook the tips of asparagus in salted water for 5 minutes. Drain, dry and marinate them for 30 minutes in oil, lemon juice and salt and pepper. Dip the asparagus in the batter and fry in deep, very hot, fat. Drain and serve at once.

ASPARAGUS IN ROLLS

Crusty bread rolls	Asparagus
Béchamel sauce	Butter

Use as many round crusty rolls as there are people. Scoop out the centres and fry the rest in butter. Make a sauce and put in it some cooked asparagus tips. When it is well cooked and very hot, pour the mixture into the rolls and serve it at once.

ASPARAGUS SOUFFLÉ

1 lb. asparagus	3 oz. butter
5 eggs	1 tbsp. flour
½ cupful milk	Salt and pepper

Cook the asparagus, but just use the tips for this recipe and the rest for soup. Cream the butter, separate the eggs and beat in the egg yolks. Beat in the sifted flour, season and beat in the milk. Whip the egg whites until they are stiff, and fold them carefully into the mixture. Add the asparagus tips and turn the whole lot into a buttered soufflé mould. Cover it with greaseproof paper and stand it in a pan of boiling water. Cook it in a moderate oven for 1 hour. Serve instantly.

ASPARAGUS TEA

Use one large handful of chopped fern to 2 cups of boiling water.

AVENS Fam. Rosaceae

Geum Urbanum
Herb Bennet

This fairly common plant grows to about 1 ft. high and has a yellow, five-petalled flower. It grows in woodlands and shaded hedgerows and prefers damp surroundings. The roots smell like cloves, and this plant was once considered a most important herb as it was used to flavour ale and prevent souring.

The young leaves are very pleasant chopped over a green salad.

BALM Fam. Labiatae

Melissa officinalis

This plant, which is a favourite of bees, is an escape which grows in woodlands in the south of England. It is hairy, yellow-green, and smells of lemon. It grows about 2 ft. high. It has small narrow white flowers which are wrinkled and look thicker than they are, on a square stem. They grow at the bases of the upper leaves. The ancient herbalist Paracelsus called this plant the elixir of life, and sold it as a cure for impotency and early ageing. The Arabs make a perfume from this plant. It contains a lot of tannin. It is a plant with definite medicinal effects, calming the nerves and stimulating the heart. Melissa tea makes a good nightcap.

The very delicate lemon flavour of the leaves makes it an excellent substitute for lemon, without the sourness of the latter. It can be added to fruit salad, ordinary green salad, fruit juices, particularly orange, goes well in iced drinks or cocktails and cups, and in China tea. It improves mayonnaise and salad dressings, herb sauces, and fish sauce. It is an excellent ingredient of stuffing with sage and imparts flavour to chicken if the bird is rubbed with fresh leaves before being roasted. It also goes well in milk puddings and milk shakes. It is an ingredient of several liqueurs. Balm can be combined with other herbs. In fact it is a very versatile, useful and tasteful herb.

BALM AND MARSHMALLOW CUSTARD

$\frac{1}{2}$ pt. milk	6 marshmallows
1 egg	$1\frac{1}{2}$ tbsp. sugar
1 tbsp. fresh balm or 1 dstp. dried leaves	1 piece vanilla pod

Put the marshmallows in a buttered fireproof dish. Beat the egg and sugar, add the milk and the cut vanilla pod. Beat all this well and pour it over the marshmallows. Sprinkle the chopped balm leaves on the top. Put the dish in a shallow pan of water and bake it slowly until set. Serve it with cream.

MELISSA TEA

Make a delicate and refreshing tea with 1 teaspoonful of leaves for each cup, and one for the pot.

BALM WINE

2 big handfuls of balm leaves	$\frac{1}{2}$ oz. yeast
2 lb. white sugar	Lemon peel (without pith)
1 gal. water	Lemon juice
1 egg white	

Boil together the water, sugar, lemon juice and beaten egg white for $\frac{1}{2}$ hour. Skim it well. Put the balm leaves in a container with the yellow peel of the lemon, and pour the boiling syrup over it. Leave it for 2 days, and then strain it into a fermentation jar. Add the yeast, and ferment to a finish before racking and bottling.

See also: Asparagus (Soup); and Metheglin (page 207).

BAY Fam. Lauraceae

Laurus nobilis

Usually an escape, big bay bushes can still be found wild, but not in extremely cold areas, or in the north. It has dark green, oval, pointed leaves, slightly lighter in colour underneath, which smell characteristically when crushed. It is easy to confuse bay with the much bigger and much more common Ilex or evergreen oak, frequently found in parklands.

Bay can be used fresh or dried, and is a most useful culinary herb. It is always part of a 'bouquet garni', and bay improves all marinades, pickles, stews and savoury dishes. It also goes well with milk dishes and custards.

The flavour of bay is so strong that it is not used by itself to make any dish, yet it is, or should be, the most used herb in any kitchen. To dry bay leaves, just hang up a branch with leaves still on it, in a well-ventilated place, and when the leaves have dried, remove them and put them in a container to preserve the flavour.

See also: Chestnut Soup 1 (page 84), and (Freshwater Fish stuffed with Chestnuts) (page 86).

BILBERRY Fam. Ericaceae

Blaeberry, Huckleberry, Whinberry, Whortleberry

This deciduous shrub which grows on heaths and moors and sometimes in woods on acid soils, is common everywhere in Britain except on its eastern side. The rarer northern bilberry grows only in the north, high up in the wet mountains and moors. The plants grow as a shrub, not more than 18 in. high, with angled green twigs. The leaves are oval and pointed

Vaccinium myrtyllus

and only very slightly toothed, and are a bright lightish green, sometimes with red tinges. The berries are small and black, and ripen in August.

Bilberries stain your fingers and tongue deep purple, so be careful not to spill juice on clothes and tablecloths. They make excellent jam, rather like blackcurrant jam, but not so seedy. Add a little apple to get a good set.

BILBERRY SOUP
1 lb. bilberries
2 oz. sugar
1½ pts. water
½ tspn. ground cinnamon

½ tbsp. cornflour
½ tspn. sweet cecily
5 oz. cream

Wash the bilberries well and put them in the water with the cinnamon, sweet cecily, and sugar, and simmer for 3 or 4 minutes until the fruit is tender. Put the whole lot through a liquidiser or a sieve. Mix the cornflour with a little of the soup; return it to the pan stirring all the time, and sweeten it to taste. Boil it again for a few moments. This soup can be eaten either hot or cold with cream added, but not stirred in, just before serving.

BILBERRY SAUCE (To eat with meat)
2 qts. bilberries
1 cup red wine
5 cloves

Pinch cinnamon
1 lb. sugar

Wash the stalked berries, drain and put them in a pan with the red wine, cloves, cinnamon and sugar. Bring it to the boil. Skim and simmer for 30 minutes. Strain off the juice, keeping the berries on one side. Go on boiling the juice until it becomes thick syrup. Put the berries back into this, and mix them well. When the purée has cooled a little, put it into jars and seal them. This is an excellent sauce to eat with cold meat or boiled beef.

STEWED BILBERRIES
Serve bilberries stewed with sugar to taste, with thin pastry fingers and plenty of thick cream.

BILBERRY PIE
1 lb. bilberries	tspn. cinnamon
4 oz. sugar	Pastry

Wash the bilberries, put them in a pie dish with the sugar and cinnamon, and make a pastry cover. Cook in a moderate oven for 25–30 minutes, and serve with cream or custard.

BILBERRY COMPOTE
2 lb. bilberries	Peel of $\frac{1}{2}$ lemon
1 lb. sugar	Pinch cinnamon
$\frac{2}{3}$ cup water	Whipped cream

Make a syrup from the sugar, water, cinnamon and lemon peel. Clean the bilberries and put them into the syrup, and boil them quickly. Put the cooked berries into a serving dish and continue cooking the syrup until it is reduced and very thick. Pour it over the fruit. Serve very cold with whipped cream.

BILBERRY CAKE
$1\frac{1}{2}$ cups bilberries	$\frac{1}{4}$ cup butter
$\frac{1}{2}$ cup sugar	1 egg
$1\frac{1}{2}$ cups flour S.R.	$\frac{1}{2}$ tspn. salt
1 cup milk	

Beat the butter and sugar until creamy, and stir in the egg yolk, milk, salt, fruit, and flour. Whisk the egg white stiffly and fold it into the mixture. Pour this into shallow well-buttered cake tin. Bake in a moderate to hot oven for about 25 minutes.

BILBERRY KISSEL (Russian recipe)

2 lb. bilberries   2½ pts. water
1 tbsp. cornflour   1 cup sugar

Pound the berries in a mortar with the water, or blend them in a blender. Put the cornflour in a pan and pour the cold juice over it, stirring all the time. Add the sugar, heat, and keep stirring. As soon as it thickens and becomes transparent, pour it into a serving bowl, and serve it piping hot with thick cream.

STEAMED BILBERRY PUDDING

Suet crust   Sugar
Bilberries

Line a pudding basin with suet crust, saving some for the lid. Fill it with the cleaned bilberries, and plenty of sugar, and cover with the rest of the suet. Cover it with a cloth, and steam for 2 hours.

BILBERRY JAM

3½ lb. bilberries   ¼ oz. tartaric acid
3 lb. sugar   ¼ pt. water

This jam never sets very hard, but can be made stiffer by adding a little pectin. Use the basic recipe on page 32.

BILBERRY AND RHUBARB JAM

3½ lb. bilberries   3½ lb. sugar
½ lb. rhubarb   Water

Wash and cut tender rhubarb, put it into the preserving pan with a little water and the sugar and boil it for 10 minutes. Add the bilberries, and simmer slowly, skimming well until the jam reaches setting point. Pour it into jars and seal in the usual way.

BILBERRY AND APPLE JELLY

Bilberries   Sugar
Apples   Water

Use equal quantities of bilberries and apples. Put the fruit into a pan and cover it with water, and boil gently for about 1 hour. Strain the fruit through a bag, stir in the sugar then boil it rapidly until the jelly is set. Seal and cover it in the usual way.

BILBERRY AND RED CURRENT JELLY

2 lb. bilberries   3 lb. sugar
1 lb. red currants

Press the berries to extract all the juice. Put this juice in a pan with the sugar and mix well. Skim it as soon as it boils and cook for 5 minutes, or until the jelly reaches setting point. Put the jelly into jars and seal them.

BILBERRY TEA

Use 1 tablespoon of young leaves to $1\frac{1}{2}$ cupsful of water.

BILBERRY JUICE

Bilberries   Water or soda water
Sugar

Squeeze the juice from the bilberries, dilute them with water or soda water and sweeten the juice to taste.

BILBERRY WINE

3 lb. bilberries   1 gal. water
3 lb. sugar   Tannin
$\frac{3}{4}$ oz. yeast   Pectic enzyme

Crush the fruit thoroughly and bring it to the boil in $\frac{2}{3}$ of the water. Leave it to stand for 2 days, add the tannin or cold tea and pectic enzyme, and make the sugar into a syrup with the rest of the water. Strain the juice into a fermentation jar, add the syrup and the yeast, and continue as usual.

To make a sweet wine, add 4 oz. of raisins, and use port type yeast. For safety add 1 Campden tablet to the must. 3 lb. of berries with 3 lb. sugar and Madeira type yeast produces a sweet dessert wine.

BIRCH Fam. Betulaceae

Betula alba
The well-known and
beautiful Silver Birch

Take birch sap from mature trees during the first 2 weeks in March. Bore a hole about 1 in. deep, slanting upwards, about 18 in. from the ground. Use a cork with a hole through the middle, insert a piece of glass tubing, and attach a piece of rubber or polythene tubing to the outside end to lead down into a collecting bottle through another cork with a hole in it. Make a small hole at one side of the cork in the jar to act as a breather and allow air out as the bottle fills. Put the first cork in the tree and in 2 days you should have collected enough sap. Be sure to cork up the hole in the tree firmly, so that no more sap can run out. The same hole can be used again the following year.

BIRCH SAP WINE 1

1 gal. juice	1 oz. almonds
3 lb. sugar	¾ oz. yeast
1 lb. raisins	

Boil the juice, sugar and raisins for 20 minutes, and when it is cool put it into a fermentation jar with the yeast. After a few days add the almonds tied in a muslin bag. When the fermentation ceases, remove the almonds and proceed in the usual way.

BIRCH SAP WINE 2

1 gal. birch sap	4 oz. raisins
2½ lb. sugar	¾ oz. yeast
1 each lemon, orange and grapefruit	½ tspn. yeast nutrient

Put all the fruit peel, without white pith, into the sap and simmer it for 10 minutes. Stir in the sugar and chopped raisins, and when the mixture is cool add the fruit juice, nutrient and yeast. Cover the container and leave it for 4 or 5 days, and then strain the liquid into a fermentation jar. Allow it to ferment to a finish, rack, mature and bottle.

BLACKBERRY Fam. Rosaceae

Robus fruticosus
Bramble

This surely needs no description, except to say that the plant is very variable. The fruit can be hard and gritty or full and luscious, and if you do find a particularly good source you can pick all the fruit you want very quickly. The great herbalist Nicholas Culpeper stated that blackberries were 'under the dominion of Venus ... and if anyone asks why Venus is so prickly, tell them it is because she is in the house of Mars'. Sufficient reason, I suppose. There are many recipes for using blackberries, but I think the finest products of the fruit are wine and bramble jelly.

The plant is also used to make teas, and an infusion of the leaves and unripe berries is good for diahorrea! The very young shoots can be picked, prepared and eaten like asparagus.

BLACKBERRY PICKLE

1 qt. blackberries	$\frac{1}{2}$ oz. ground ginger
2 lb. sugar	$1\frac{1}{2}$ oz. allspice
1 pt. white vinegar	

Steep the blackberries and ginger in the vinegar for 12 hours. Strain and retain the fruit and bring the vinegar to the boil, add the berries and sugar, and simmer it for $\frac{1}{2}$ hour. When it is cold, add the spice, mix everything well together, put it in jars and cover.

BLACKBERRY VINEGAR

3 lb. blackberries	1 qt. white or
Sugar	malt vinegar

Pour the vinegar over the blackberries and leave them to stand for 8 days. Then strain them, put the liquid in a pan and boil it for 5 minutes. Add 1 lb. sugar to each pint of liquid and heat it until the sugar is dissolved. Cool and bottle it. This can be used as a hot drink in water, or as a sort of gravy poured over Yorkshire pudding.

APPLES STUFFED WITH BLACKBERRIES

Apples	Sugar or golden
Blackberries	syrup

Peel and core the apples and put them in a pie dish. Press the blackberries to a pulp and mix them with sugar or golden syrup. Push this down in the openings of the apples and spread the rest round them. Add just enough water to prevent scorching, cover with foil and cook them in a moderate oven until the apples are done.

BLACKBERRY AND CRAB APPLE PUDDING

$\frac{1}{2}$ large sliced loaf	1 lb. blackberries
6 oz. sugar	$\frac{1}{2}$ pint water
$\frac{3}{4}$ lb. crab apples	

Cut the crusts off the slices of bread (which can be rather stale), and carefully line a bowl with them, making sure they completely cover its surface. Dissolve the sugar in the water and bring it to the boil and put in the blackberries. Cook them for a few minutes only, then strain them off. In the same liquid cook the sliced and peeled crab apples to a pulp. Check that they are sweet enough, as crab apples can be very sour. Put the blackberries back in with the apples and mix them well together before turning the whole lot into the bread-lined bowl. Cover the top of the fruit with another layer of bread, put a saucer or lid over the top to fit exactly, and weight it down. Leave the pudding overnight in the fridge, and serve it the next day with masses of cream.

POTTED BLACKBERRIES

4 lb. blackberries	1 oz. butter
4 lb. sugar	

Heat the sugar in a bowl in a warm oven. Grease the preserving pan with a little butter and put the berries in it over a low heat. When they bubble, pour in the sugar. Beat it with a wooden spoon for 30 minutes, over a very low heat making sure that the mixture does not stick or burn. Put it into jars and seal them.

BRAMBLE AND ROSE HIP JAM

Blackberries	Butter (unsalted)
Rose hips	Water
Sugar	

Use a large cupful of hips to each 3 lb. of blackberries. Cut the hips, remove the seeds, chop the fruits small and leave them to stand, just covered with water, for 2 days. Pick the blackberries, wash them and put them into the bowl with the hips. Stand them for a few hours in a very cool oven to extract the juice. Butter the preserving pan and empty the fruit and juice into it, adding 1 lb. of sugar to each pint, stirring until the sugar dissolves. Boil the jam quickly until it is set, skim it and put it in jars.

BLACKBERRY AND APPLE MARMALADE

Blackberries   Sugar

Apples   Water

Wash the apples but do not peel or core them. Put the apples and washed blackberries into a pan. Just cover them with water. Bring them to the boil, and when the fruit is all a pulp, rub it through a sieve. To every 1 lb. of pulp, add 1 lb. sugar. Boil it again for ½ hour, stirring constantly. Put into jars and seal.

SPICED BRAMBLE JELLY

Blackberries   Nutmeg

Sugar   Mace

Water   Cinnamon

Wash the blackberries, and cover them with water in a preserving pan. Add a saltspoonful of mixed nutmeg, mace and cinnamon to each 1 lb. of fruit. Bring it all to the boil and simmer it until the juice is extracted. Put it in a jelly bag and leave it until the next day. Add 1 lb. of sugar to each pint of juice and boil it rapidly for 30 minutes. Put it into jars and seal.

BLACKBERRY WINE

1 gal. blackberries   ¾ oz. yeast

3 lb. sugar   1 lemon

1 gal. water   1 Campden tablet

Wash the berries and put them in a large container. Boil the water and pour it over the fruit. Add the Campden tablet. Cover, and let it stand for a week, stirring daily. Do not mash it. Make a syrup with some of the juice and the sugar, and when it is cool, strain the rest of the juice into it and put it all into fermentation jars with the lemon juice. Add the yeast. Ferment to a finish, rack, mature and bottle.

BLACKBERRY LIQUEUR

3 lb. blackberries   2 cloves

1 qt. brandy   Small piece cinnamon

3 lb. white sugar   bark

Wash the fruit and mash it thoroughly. Add the spices to make a strong tasty liqueur. Steep it all in the brandy for 3 days, then strain and press out all the liquor. Put the sugar in a saucepan with just enough water to stop it burning, and dissolve it carefully. When this syrup is cold, add it to the other liquid. Leave it for a few hours, stir it thoroughly, strain and bottle it. It is ready to drink at once.

FORTIFIED BLACKBERRY SYRUP (LIQUEUR)

1 lb. blackberries	1 tbsp. brandy
1 lb. white sugar	1 tbsp. cold water

Put the fruit, sugar and water together in a container with a cover, and stand this in a saucepan of boiling water and simmer it for 2 hours. Strain the juice, boil it in a saucepan for 20 minutes, skimming off any rubbish, Allow the syrup to cool and add the brandy. Bottle it and use it fairly quickly.

See also: Cottage Cheese with Strawberries (page 188) which can also be made with blackberries.

See Sloe and Blackberry Jelly (page 61); Elderberry and Blackberry Jam (page 114).

BLACKTHORN Fam. Rosaceae

Prunus spinosa
Sloe

This is a very common hedgerow shrub, characterised by its lovely white blossom which appears in April before the leaves, making a wonderful contrast with the dark spiky twigs. Small oval leaves appear as the flowers fall, followed in autumn by the little black plums, covered with purple bloom. Bite into one of these at your peril, for they are so bitter and sour that the whole mouth seems to dry up. Nevertheless this fruit has a fine flavour and is one that we neglect, for it has many uses.

With apples or blackberries it makes a fine jelly, and it is a good wine fruit. Best of all is sloe gin, a liqueur which if carefully made, not too sweet, retains the astringent flavour of the fresh fruit.

SLOE AND APPLE JELLY

4 lb. apples
1 lb. sugar to every
    pint of juice

2 lb. sloes
Water to cover

Wash the apples and cut them up. Put them in a pan with the sloes, washed and de-stalked. Cover with water and boil it all to a pulp. Strain it through a cloth without squeezing. Measure the liquid and put it back in the pan with 1 lb. of sugar for every pint of juice. Boil it for 15 minutes, fill the pots and seal them.

To vary this recipe use equal quantities of sloes and apples. Or 3 lb. sloes to 1 lb. apples. But use $1\frac{1}{2}$ lb. sugar to every pint of juice.

Any of these jellies are excellent with mutton, hare or rabbit.

SLOE AND BLACKBERRY JELLY

2 lb. sloes
8 lb. blackberries

5 lb. sugar
3 pts. water

Boil the fruit well in the water then strain it well through double muslin or a sieve, extracting all the juice. To each 7 pts. juice add 5 lb. sugar, and boil it quickly for about $\frac{1}{2}$ hour. Put the jelly in jars and seal them.

SLOE WINE

3 lb. ripe sloes
$2\frac{3}{4}$ lb. sugar
1 gal. water

$\frac{1}{2}$ tspn. yeast nutrient
1 Campden tablet
$\frac{3}{4}$ oz. yeast

Clean and stalk the sloes, but leave the pips. Pour the boiling water over them and mash them well the next day. Leave covered for 2 days then strain them. Make a syrup with the sugar and half the juice, and when it is cool, add the nutrient and yeast and put it into a fermentation jar. Ferment to a finish, rack, mature and bottle.

SLOE GIN

Ripe sloes	White sugar
Almonds	Gin

Half fill any big jar with a good sealing top with sloes. Add $\frac{1}{2}$ lb. sugar and 4 or 5 blanched (skinned) almonds to each $\frac{1}{2}$ lb. of fruit, and top the lot up with gin. Screw down the jar, and shake the contents thoroughly. Reverse the jar every 2 or 3 days. After 2 months, strain and bottle the liquid. The longer you keep it the better it is, but it usually gets drunk up rather quickly!

BOG MYRTLE Fam. Myricaceae

Myrica gale
Candleberry, Sweet Gale

A shrub which grows on boggy moors and heaths and in fens. Once protected by law in this country, it grows about 4 ft. high and has a reddish stem. Orange male and red female catkins appear before the leaves on separate plants. The plant secretes wax from glands under the leaves which give it a wonderful resinous smell. Once the leaves used to be mashed in hot water to free the wax which was then made into sweet-smelling candles.

The small two-winged fruits can be used as a flavouring for soup, and small amounts of the fruits and leaves added to meat stews give them an interesting flavour. This is a plant with which to experiment. I have been unable to try it, but perhaps a few fruits added to a basic home made white wine might produce something resembling the Greek white wine Retsina, which tastes so strongly of resin.

BORAGE Fam. Boraginaceae

Borago officinalis

The Romans brought borage to Britain and it grows wild on the chalk downs of southern England. It grows to 3 ft. high and the whole plant, leaves and stem, is covered with coarse hairs. The flowers grow in loose spikes and are a wonderful dark sky blue, with dark maroon anthers. It flowers in June.

Borage flowers can be candied (see page 168).

The leaves are added to long cool drinks, cocktails and cups, to give a flavour of cucumber, and have a slightly stimulating effect.

The chopped leaves are quite good in salad, but the best use for this is as a flavouring for natural yoghurt or cream cheese. The leaves must be chopped fairly small and mixed in to taste, otherwise their hairiness makes them unpalatable.

They can also be eaten raw, chopped, between pieces of bread and butter.
See also: Dandelion – Pissenlit au Lard (Dandelion Salad).

BROOKLIME Fam. Scrophulariaceae

Veronica beccabunga

A common plant in very wet places, brooklime has large round smooth fleshy leaves and small blue flowers growing up the stem at the base of the leaves. The leaves are good additions to salads, but do be sure that they are clean and that the water from which they have been gathered is not contaminated.

BROOM Fam. Papilionaceae

Sarothamnus scoparius

This almost hairless deciduous shrub, which looks rather like gorse without prickles, grows everywhere on dry acid soils, particularly heaths. The bright yellow flowers, sometimes tinged with red, grow all the way up the angled stems, and bloom in May and June. The leaves are small and thin.

BROOM WINE

1 gal. broom flowers	2 oranges
1 gal. water	$\frac{3}{4}$ oz. yeast
3 lb. white sugar	$\frac{1}{2}$ tspn. yeast nutrient
2 lemons	

Boil the sugar and water together with the rinds of the citrus fruits (without the white pith). When it has cooled pour it over the flowers, add the lemon and orange juice, and the nutrient, and last the yeast. After 2 days strain the liquid into a fermentation jar.

Or pour boiling water over the flowers and rinds and leave the must to stand, well covered, for 2 days. Then add the other ingredients (except the yeast) and strain the must into the fermentation jar. Add the yeast and ferment it to a finish. Rack, mature and bottle.

BULLACE Fam. Rosaceae

Prunus domestica
Wild Plum

Bullaces, plums, greengages, damsons, etc., escape and grow wild, and odd trees can frequently be found in the country-side, especially where houses have been pulled down perhaps many years ago, and traces of the gardens remain. The twigs,

C

sometimes thorny, are dull grey or brown, and the leaves also are dull. These trees are often hard for the amateur to identify, but are very like sloe or blackthorn. The fruit is always edible and can be cooked by any of the recipes for the domesticated varieties of the fruit, although more sugar is usually necessary.

BULLACE CHEESE
Bullaces   Sugar

Wash the fruit, cook it to a pulp and put it through a sieve or blender. Weigh the purée and add ¾ lb. of sugar to every 1 lb. of pulp. Boil it, stirring carefully until it is set. Put the jam into jars and seal them.

BULLACE WINE
4 lb. bullaces   ½ tspn. yeast nutrient
3 lb. white sugar   or ½ lb. raisins
1 gal. water   1 Campden tablet
¼ oz. baker's yeast   Pecotzyme

Pour boiling water over the fruit, and mash it well. Leave it covered for 3 or 4 days. Make a syrup with the sugar and half the strained juice. Add the other ingredients and put the must into fermentation jars. If raisins are used, chop them and put them into the jar before adding the liquid. Ferment to a finish, rack, mature and bottle.

BULRUSH Fam. Typhaceae

Typha latifolia
False Bulrush, Common Reedmace

So common and well known as to need no description, except to say that be sure it is the great bulrush and not the lesser bulrush which has more grass-like leaves and milk-chocolate-coloured flowers, whereas the bulrush flower spike is chocolate brown, almost black, and bigger.

The young sprouts and shoots, especially the white insides can be eaten as salad. In some countries bulrush pollen is used as a flavouring, and various other parts of the roots and unripe flower heads are boiled as vegetables.

BURNET Fam. Rosaceae

Poterium sanguisorba
Salad Burnet

A small plant with greenish globular flowers with yellow stamens low down. The leaves are deeply indented and grow in pairs opposite each other up the stem. The fruits are four-sided, divided by practically straight ridges. The plant is common in England in grassy places on chalk, but more local in Scotland and Ireland. Salad burnet smells faintly of cucumber when crushed, and has rather the same flavour.

BURNET WINE

2 qts. burnet heads	3 lb. sugar
2 lb. sugar	3 qts. flower heads
1 gal. water	½ lb. chopped raisins
1 lemon	½oz. root ginger
1 orange	1 gal. water
¾ oz. yeast	1 lemon
or :	1 orange
	¾ oz. yeast

Pour half the boiling water over the flower heads and leave it to stand for 24 hours. Make a syrup with the rest of the water, add the lemon and orange, sliced but with the white pith removed. After 24 hours, strain the juice from the flowers into the syrup, add the yeast, put it into fermentation jars, and continue as usual.

To make a heavier wine, proceed as above, adding chopped raisins and bruised ginger to the contents of the fermentation jar. Pour off into another jar after 3 weeks, discarding the raisins and ginger. Continue as usual.

CABBAGE (WILD) Fam. Cruciferae

Brassica oleracea

Around the south-eastern corner of England on the white cliffs of Dover there grows in profusion what is locally known as Cliff Cabbage. This looks very like sprouting broccoli and produces yellow flowers. It is reputed to be an escape from the kitchen gardens of the Roman settlers. Wild cabbage – *Brassica oleracea*, is the original plant from which many of the cultived 'greens' sprang and is a scarce plant, but several varieties of cabbage and kale can be found wild in this country and they are all escapes from somewhere. They are, of course, perfectly edible, and often have a far superior flavour to the cultivated varieties. The cabbage which grows on the cliffs is full of flavour, and the young flower-bearing sprouts picked while still purplish green, with their surrounding leaves, should be boiled lightly in a little salted water, and served with melted butter are a delicious vegetable. Use just enough water to prevent the vegetable from burning, and by the time it is tender but not mushy, almost all the water should have boiled away. Don't chop up the cabbage, either before or after cooking, but serve it entire in its pieces. These various cabbages can be cooked by any recipe used for the cultivated varieties.

WILD CABBAGE SOUP
½ lb. wild cabbage
2 sliced potatoes

2 tbsp. olive oil
2 pts. chicken stock

When the stock is boiling, add drop by drop, the olive oil and then the sliced potatoes. Cook them until they are soft, then mash them roughly. Slice the cabbage leaves as finely as possible and put them in the boiling broth for 2 or 3 minutes, then serve the soup instantly.

WILD CABBAGE AND OATMEAL
1 lb. wild cabbage
Oatmeal
Cream

Salt and pepper
Water

Put the cabbage in a pan with a little salted water, and cook it until it is quite tender. Drain it thoroughly and chop it finely, then rub it through a sieve. Put this purée back into the pan with a little extra water if it is very thick, add a sprinkling of oatmeal, simmer it for a few minutes, and season it with salt and pepper. Stir in a little cream just before serving.

WILD CABBAGE, POTATOES AND SAUSAGES

1 lb. wild cabbage	1 oz. butter
1 lb. mashed potato	Salt and pepper
Smoked sausage	

Clean and boil the wild cabbage until it is quite tender. Drain, chop and mix it with the mashed potato. Add salt and pepper to taste and stir in the butter. Put all this in an oven dish and cover it with a layer of thinly sliced smoked sausage. Heat it in a moderate oven until the sausage slices are hot.

WILD CABBAGE AND YOGHURT

Wild cabbage	Butter
Carton of yoghurt	Paprika
Breadcrumbs	Salt

Wash, chop and boil the cabbage in salted water. Butter a pie dish and put in a layer of cabbage, with a little yoghurt on top. Repeat this process ending with the yoghurt. Sprinkle breadcrumbs, paprika and butter on the top and brown it in the oven.

CALAMINT Fam. Labiatae

Calamintha officinalis

Calamint grows in England, Wales and southern Ireland, and is plentiful locally especially on chalk and limestone. It grows about 2 ft. high and has spikes of pale violet flowers spotted darker, in short, opposite clusters at the bases of the small, slightly toothed, dark green leaves. The whole plant has a minty smell. It can be used as a flavouring herb as a substitute for mint or basil.

CARAWAY Fam. Umbelliferae

Carum carvi

Caraway grows to about 1 ft. high has hollow stems, leaves opposite each other and umbrellas of white flowers. These turn to oblong rigid fruits which have the distinctive caraway seed smell. When the fruits are ripe they tend to shatter, so are best harvested in the early morning when still damp with dew. The seeds are larger than anise seeds, although they look alike and share the flavour of liquorice. They can be used to flavour cheese and biscuits, and to sprinkle on home-made bread.

CARAWAY SOUP

3 pts. beef broth	1 tbsp. caraway seeds
Flour	Gravy browning
Mixed vegetables	Butter
(onions, carrots,	Croutons
tomatoes, etc.,)	Salami sausage

Boil the mixed vegetables in the stock with the caraway seeds until they are tender. Strain the liquid and thicken it with a flour and butter roux. Add a little gravy browning, stirring it until smooth. Serve the soup with croutons of bread and diced salami sausage.

PORK CHOPS IN CARAWAY CREAM SAUCE

1 pork chop, chump chop, or leg fillet per person	Butter Plain flour Paprika
1 tspn. caraway seeds per chop	Salt and pepper Spatzle or yellow noodles
Stock or home-made white wine	Green salad

Brown the chops lightly in the butter and put them in a fire-proof dish. Sprinkle the caraway seeds all over them and pour on enough stock or wine to cover the chops. Put a lid on the dish or cover it with baking foil. Put it in a slow oven for about an hour until the chops are tender. Make a roux with 1 oz. butter and a dessertspoonful flour. Add the gravy from the chops to this, stirring all the time. The sauce should be the consistency of thick cream. Add enough paprika to make the sauce pink, and season it to taste. If it does not taste strongly enough of caraway, add a few more seeds and cook the sauce for a minute or two longer. Pour the sauce back over the chops and serve with spatzle, if obtainable, or any small yellow noodles, and a mixed green salad.

CARAWAY POTATOES WITH COTTAGE CHEESE

2 lb. small potatoes	Butter
8 oz. cottage cheese	2-3 tbsp. milk or cream
Caraway seeds	Salt

Wash the potatoes carefully and halve them. Dip each cut side into the caraway seeds and salt, so that it is well coated. Place them on a greased baking dish, seed side up. Brush them with melted butter and bake them in a moderate oven until tender. Blend the cheese and milk or cream carefully and serve it as a separate sauce with the potatoes. Philadelphia cream cheese with added milk can be used for the sauce instead of cottage cheese.

CARAWAY DUMPLINGS

8 oz. S.R. flour	2 tspn. caraway seeds
6 oz. suet	$\frac{1}{4}$ pt. water
1 small grated onion	Salt

Mix all the dry ingredients, then add the water and make a stiff dough. Make small dumplings out of this and drop them into boiling stock of the dish they are to be served with. Cook them for 20 minutes, and serve immediately.

CARAWAY AND ONION SAUCE

1 pt. stock	2–3 onions
$1\frac{1}{2}$ oz. butter	Sugar and vinegar to
$1\frac{1}{2}$ oz. plain flour	taste
1 tspn. caraway seeds	Salt

Melt the butter, add the flour and finely chopped onions and cook them until golden. Add the stock, stirring all the time, then add the caraway seeds. Bring the sauce to the boil and simmer it for 10 minutes. Rub it through a sieve and season it with salt, sugar and vinegar.

TIPPERARY SEED CAKE

1 lb. butter	1 lb. S.R. flour
Orange flower water	$\frac{1}{2}$ lb. almonds
$1\frac{1}{2}$ lb. castor sugar	2 oz. caraway seeds
16 eggs	

Mash the butter in the orange flower water and beat it to a cream. Mix in the sugar and well beaten eggs. Add the flour, beating all the time. Blanch and pound the almonds, or use ground almonds. Add these and the caraway seeds and keep on beating for $\frac{1}{2}$ hour, or its equivalent if using an electric mixer. Pour the mixture into a buttered tin lined with buttered paper, and bake in a quick oven for 2 hours.

SEED CAKE (Rich)

$\frac{3}{4}$ lb. butter	1 lb. S.R. flour
6 eggs	$\frac{3}{4}$ oz. caraway seeds
$\frac{3}{4}$ lb. castor sugar	Mace and nutmeg

Beat the butter until it is creamy and add the sugar, mace and nutmeg to taste, caraway seeds, beating them well in. Gradually add the whisked eggs and mix in the flour, using a little milk if the mixture is too stiff. Put it all into a paper-lined cake tin and bake from 1½ to 2 hours in a moderate oven.

CARAWAY CORDIAL

1 oz. caraway seeds	1 pt. strong syrup
1 pt. brandy	(see page 25)

Steep the caraway seeds in the brandy for a fortnight, then strain them off and add the syrup. Bottle.

CARAWAY WINE

1 oz. caraway seeds	3 lemons
2 lb. gooseberries	3 lb. sugar
1 lb. crushed wheat	½ tspn. yeast nutrient
½ pt. cold tea	¾ oz. yeast
1 gal. water	

See also: Metheglin (page 207); and Coriander (Cordial).

CARRAGEEN Fam. Rhodophyceae

Chondrus crispus
Irish Moss, Sea Moss

Purplish-red seaweed which goes green in strong sunlight. It forms clusters of 10 to 20 fronds which grow from a discoid holdfast about ½ in. in diameter. The basal growth of carrageen is narrow and compressed, gradually spreading out to a frond which is flat and branched 6 to 8 times. Sometimes the thallus or 'leaf' grows wide and makes the plant look fan-shaped, but other types do not broaden in this way. Both forms reach 3 or 4 in. long before they begin to divide. The tips of the branches are obtuse to subacute – notched. Carrageen grows on rocks or stones and is common round the Irish coast.

Gather carragen in rock pools at low tide in April and May. Wash it carefully in sea water until it is clean. Cut off the roots and dark stems, and spread the seaweed on the grass so that the dew will fall on it. It is best bleached in showery weather. If there is no rain, sprinkle the seaweed with water frequently, and it will gradually change colour from brown, through beetroot, to pink and finally to a creamy white with pink edges. This will take several days. Then put the carrageen on a window sill or in a greenhouse so that it dries in the sun as quickly as possible. Store it in paper bags or in jars.

Some cooks use carrageen without bleaching it, but it tastes very strongly of iodine and sea, and is therefore very much an acquired taste.

CARRAGEEN MOULD

½ oz. carrageen	Lemon rind or bay
1½ pts. milk	leaf
1 egg	Salt
1 tbsp. sugar	

Wash the carrageen and steep it for ½ hour in fresh water. Pour it into a saucepan with the milk and a little salt. Add some lemon rind. (In the Hebrides where this is a traditional dish, the islanders do not add any extra flavouring, but instead of the lemon rind, the juice of 2 Seville oranges, or a stick of cinnamon help to disguise the sea taste and give extra flavour.) Bring the liquid to the boil and let it simmer slowly for about 20 minutes until it is thick. Add the sugar and stir it in. Strain the liquid over a beaten egg, return it to the pan and cook it without boiling for a minute or two. Pour it through a sieve into a wetted mould or bowl. When it is set, turn it out and serve it with fresh or slightly sour cream.

CARRAGEEN PUDDING

Carrageen	Egg
Milk	Wine

This is very similar to the previous recipe and the same quantities should be used. Pour the boiling milk over the carrageen and let it stand in a hot place without actually boiling. Add a well-beaten egg and a little wine, but again, do not let it boil. When it has cooled and set, serve it with cream.

CARRAGEEN SOUFFLE

½ oz. carrageen	1 tbsp. sherry
1 pt. milk	1 oz. sugar
½ pt. whipped cream	Chopped nuts
1 egg	

Soak the carrageen in water for 10 minutes then put it with the milk into a saucepan and cook it until it thickens. Beat the egg yolk and pour the strained carrageen and milk over it, and whisk it until it starts to set. Add the sugar and sherry. Very carefully stir in the stiffly whisked egg white and cream and put the mixture in a soufflé dish. It is worth the trouble to put paper round the dish and then when it is quite set and cold, remove this carefully, so the pudding stands up on its own above the rim of the dish. Cream and chopped nuts make the decoration.

CARRAGEEN DRINK

½ oz. carrageen	Sugar and flavouring
3 pts. milk, or milk and water	to taste

Simmer the carrageen and milk very slowly for 4 to 5 hours. Extra flavourings and sugar can be added according to taste. Strain the liquid before serving it.

CATMINT Fam. Labiatae

This plant grows on hedgebanks and roadsides in southern Britain, but is not very plentiful. It has a minty smell which cats adore, as they do that of garden catmint, which is a different plant. It is a tough little plant growing up to 2 ft. high, the greyish-green heart-shaped and toothed leaves being covered with whitish down. The white flowers have red dots, and grow in dense whorls at the top of the stem. Catmint tea is a very pleasant drink, though it is a cultivated taste. The

Nepeta cataria

leaves can be added to stews, and the young shoots are palatable in salads.

CELERY Fam. Umbelliferae

Apium graveolens

Wild celery grows in wet places near the sea, and is at its best from June to August. It is easily identified by its celery smell, and has leaves which look just like cultivated celery. The flowers are white, in umbels with short stalks. All the plant can be used, from seed to root, but the wild variety does not have the thick white stalks of the blanched cultivated plant. It is an excellent salad plant and all of it can be eaten raw. It makes a first class flavouring for sauces, stews, soups, in fact any dish where cultivated celery would be used. Braised with butter and a little chicken stock and salt, in a fireproof dish it makes an excellent hot vegetable. The leaves of the plant can be cut at any time. They should be cooked separately in a little water before serving.

Wild celery can be bitter and indigestible as it has not, like cultivated celery, been blanched, so try a little to see if it agrees with you before using large quantities.

CREAM OF CELERY SOUP

1 cupful celery stems and a few leaves	1 shallot
1 oz. butter	Milk
1 tbsp. plain flour	Salt and pepper

Chop the celery stalks and the shallot and sauté them till golden in butter. Stir in the flour, then add the milk very gradually, stirring all the time, keeping the pan over the heat as the mixture thickens. Go on adding milk until the consistency is right. Season with salt and black pepper. Chop a few celery leaves small and sprinkle them on each plateful of soup as served. A little grated Parmesan cheese can also be added.

CELERY AND MUSHROOM FRY

1 lb. chopped celery	2 tbsp. soy sauce
½ lb. mushrooms	1 tspn. sugar
2 tbsp. olive oil	Salt to taste

Wash the mushrooms and wild celery and chop them both into small pieces. Fry the mushrooms in the oil for a couple of minutes. Add the soy sauce, salt and sugar and then the celery. Cook all this for 5 minutes, then serve.

BAKED CLERY

Wild celery	Butter
1 egg	Salt and pepper
½ pt. milk	Grated cheese
Water	

Boil the celery for 10 minutes, drain it and put it in a small casserole with the milk, knob of butter, and salt and pepper. Cook it until tender, and let it cool. Beat the egg with the cool liquid, and pour this over the celery. Put it in a cool oven, cooking it until the custard turns light brown. Serve with a little grated cheese sprinkled on top.

CELERY WINE

4 lb. celery leaves and stalks	2 lemons
1 gal. water	1 orange
2½ lb. sugar	¾ oz. dried yeast
	½ tspn. yeast nutrient

Cut the celery into small pieces and add the thin rinds of the fruit without the white pith. Cover with the water and bring it to the boil, simmering gently until the celery is tender. Strain the liquid on to the sugar and stir it well until the sugar is all dissolved. Add the juice of the citrus fruit when the liquid has cooled. Then strain the must into fermentation jars and add the yeast nutrient and yeast. Ferment to a finish, rack, mature and bottle.

To alter the flavour a little, boil 1 oz. bruised root ginger with the celery, and use 3½ lb. sugar. This makes a much sweeter, heavier wine.

See also: Mushrooms (Mushroom and Wild Celery Pie); Crab apple (and Wild Celery Curry); Chestnuts (Braised); Horseradish (Cole Slaw); Sorrel (Cold Sorrel Soup); Violets (Salad); and Hot Sauce (page 205).

CHAMOMILE Fam. Compositae

A feathery leaved plant with daisy-like flowers which smell of sweet apples. It spreads along the ground thickly enough to make turf. It has no down beneath the leaves and prefers sandy soils. Chamomile flowers from June to August, and was once popular for lawns in gardens. It grows where grass would dry out from drought and smells good when crushed underfoot.

The French, and Peter Rabbit's mother, are particularly fond of chamomile tea.

Matricaria chamomilla
Scented Mayweed

Anthemis nobilis
Chamomile

CHAMOMILE TEA

½ oz. dried chamomile   2 pts. water

Pour the boiling water over the leaves and let it stand for 5 to 10 minutes before pouring it out and drinking it.

CHAMOMILE WINE

20 chamomile flowers   3 lemons
4 lb. carrots   ½ pt. tea
3½ lb. sugar   ½ tspn. yeast nutrient
1 gal. water   ¾ oz. yeast

This recipe makes a fairly sweet, fairly heavy, white wine, taking its colour from the carrots.

Clean, slice and boil the carrots in the water until they are tender, and strain them on to the sugar. Pour a little boiling water on to the chamomile flowers and let them steep for a day. Add this strained liquid to the must with the lemon juice, cold tea, nutrient and yeast, and pour it all into a fermentation jar. Ferment to a finish, rack, mature and bottle.

See also: Highland Bitters (page 208)

CHERRY (WILD) Fam. Rosaceae

Prunus avium Gean
P. cerasus
Wild Morello Cherry

Wild cherry is a tall deciduous tree with smooth, shiny, red-brown bark which peels horizontally across the trunk. The pointed oval leaves are coppery in the spring, turning redder as the season progresses, and they hang downwards. The flowers are white, in clusters, and bloom in April and May. The berries in late autumn are red, just like small cultivated cherries. The tree is common in the south in hedgerows and woods and is often associated with beech woods and oak woods.

The fruit can be used for any recipes for cultivated cherry, provided that the amount of sugar is adjusted to compensate if the wild crop happens to be sour.

'To make Cherry Water: Take nine pounds of cherries, pull out the stones and stalks, break them with your hand, and put them into nine pintes of Claret Wine, take nine ounces of Cinnamon, and three Nutmegs, Bruise them, and put them into this, then take of Rosemary and Balm of each a handfull, of sweet Marjoram and a quarter of a handfull: put all these with the aforementioned into a earthen pot well leaded, so let them start to infuse four hours, stirring it once in four or five hours; so distill it in a Limbeck keeping the strongest water by it self, put some Sugar finely beaten into your glasses. If your first water to be too strong, put some of your second to it as you use it. If you please you may tye some Musk and Ambergreece in a rag, and hang it by a thread in your glass.'

W.M., *The Queen's Closet Opened,* 1655.

WILD CHERRY SOUP

1 lb. stoned cherries	Lemon peel
1 cup water	Sugar to taste
Cinnamon bark	1 cup red wine
1 tbsp. dried potato	

Put the cherries, water, cinnamon and lemon peel in a saucepan and cook them briskly for 10 minutes. Press the cherries through a fine sieve, or put them through a blender. Dilute this with the wine which has been boiled with the crushed cherry stones, then strained. Mix it all and thicken it with the dried potato. Stir in the sugar and serve it at once.

CHERRY JAM

Cherries	Gooseberry or
Water	currant juice
Sugar	

Weigh the cherries, stone them and put them into a preserving pan. Cover them with water and boil until nearly all the liquid has gone (about ¾ hour). Add sugar, allowing 1 lb. to every 6 lb. fruit, and gooseberry or currant juice, allowing 1 pint to every 6 lb. Boil all together until it jellies (20 to 30 minutes), skimming it well, and stirring to stop it sticking. Put it into pots and seal them.

WILD CHERRY LIQUEUR

4 lb. cherries	½ lb. sugar
1 pt. brandy	

Crush the cherries and stones and put them all in a bowl to ferment for 4 days. Add the brandy, put the mixture into a jar with the sugar and leave it to infuse for a month. Squeeze it through a fine cloth and bottle it.

CHERRY LIQUEUR

4 pts. brandy	1 tspn. cinnamon
¼ lb. cherry stone kernels	10 to 12 cloves
⅓ oz. peach blossom or leaves	1 lb. sugar
	4 pts. cherry juice

Put the brandy, blanched cherry stone kernels, peach blossom or leaves, cinnamon, and cloves in a bowl, mix them well and leave them for a week. Then pour over this the cherry juice with the sugar dissolved in it. Mix it well, strain and bottle it.

CHERRY WINE

4 lb. wild cherries	Nutrient
1 gal. water	Pectozyme
3½ lb. demerara sugar	¾ oz. yeast
Campden tablet	

Clean and stalk the cherries, pour boiling water over them, and when cool mash well and add 1 tspn. of pectozyme and a Campden tablet. Leave covered for 2 days, then strain and press. Stir in the sugar, nutrient and yeast. Pour into fermentation jars, ferment to a finish, rack, mature and bottle.

CHERRY STONE LIQUEUR

1 lb. wild cherry stones	1 pt. brandy
	½ lb. sugar

This liqueur is made the same way as the recipe above. The stones used can be those left over from making cherry jam.

CHERRY BRANDY

Morello cherries	Blanched almonds
Sugar (castor)	Brandy

Half fill a big Kilner jar with cherries, and add ½ lb. sugar. Top up the jar with brandy and put in 6 blanched almonds. Screw the jar down tightly and shake it well, put it somewhere accessible, and every time you pass it, turn the jar the other way up. After 3 months it will be fit to strain, bottle and drink. See also: Summer Pudding (page 105).

CHESTNUT (SPANISH OR SWEET) Fam. Fagaceae

'The chestnut is for the man who takes its shell off.'
Italian proverb.

Spanish chestnut grows abundantly in the southern half of England, either as single trees or in woodlands, usually cop-

Castanea sativa

piced, although where the trees have been left to grow un-
hindered the nuts are usually bigger and more plentiful. Unlike horse chestnut (which is totally different) it neither has
leaves spread out like a hand nor candles of flowers, but has
large shiny pointed leaves with saw-toothed edges. The nuts
are inside very prickly green cases. If they fall when fully
ripe the cases burst open and the nuts are scattered, but most
nuts come down still firmly shut in cases, and you need a stout
pair of gloves to get them out. After the cases have lain on
the ground for a while they dry out and open and spill the
nuts. Chestnuts are such a good source of food that in some
Mediterranean countries they are a staple, often dried and
ground into flour. Several recipes for using this flour are given
below.

The traditional British way to eat chestnuts is to roast them.
Make a slit to let out steam as they heat up, or the nuts may
explode. Roast them close to an open fire or in an oven. It is
difficult to get the nuts out without burning your fingers, but
worth it. For all recipes, chestnuts must have both out and
inner skin removed and they can be boiled or put in the oven
and allowed to cool a little before being peeled.

CHESTNUT SOUP 1

1 lb. chestnuts	1 bayleaf
1 potato	Egg yolk
1 pt. stock	Salt and pepper
½ pt. milk	Top of the milk

Shell and skin the chestnuts and put them in a pan with the stock, diced potato, bayleaf and salt and pepper. Simmer until it is all tender, sieve it, or put it through a blender, add the milk and reheat it. Just before serving stir in an egg yolk mixed with a little top of the milk. Don't let the soup boil once the egg is in.

CHESTNUT SOUP 2

½ lb. peeled chestnuts	Rind of 1 orange
1 bar plain chocolate	2 tbsp. castor sugar
8 tbsp. dark brown sugar	Little ground cinnamon
	Little nutmeg
4 tbsp. chocolate powder	2–3 cloves
	1 tbsp. rum
Rind of 1 lemon	

Skin and peel the chestnuts in the usual way. Put them and all the ingredients except the rum in a casserole with enough water to cover them, and simmer it all until the chestnuts are quite tender. Remove the orange and lemon rind and the cloves before adding the rum, and serve it piping hot.

GREEK CHESTNUT STUFFING (for turkey)

1½ lb. chestnuts	3 oz. sultanas
1 lb. minced veal	1 tbsp. sugar
1 onion	Cinnamon
3 oz. pine nuts	Butter
¼ pt. tomato juice	Salt and pepper

Boil and peel the chestnuts keeping them as whole as possible. Slice and fry the onion in butter until it is golden, then add the minced veal and cook it for a few minutes. Add the tomato juice, sugar, salt, pepper and cinnamon. Stir this all for a few moments then carefully mix in the chestnuts, pine nuts and sultanas. When the mixture is cool enough to handle, stuff the turkey with it.

CHESTNUT STUFFING 2 (For turkey or chicken)

2 lb. chestnuts	Juice of 1 lemon
¼ lb. butter	Port
1 beaten egg	Salt

Slit and boil the chestnuts until they are soft, then peel and skin them. For a very fine stuffing, sieve the chestnuts, for a medium stuffing, put them through a coarse mincer, for chunky stuffing, just chop the nuts with a knife. Melt the butter, add it to the chestnuts and mix well. Add lemon juice and a pinch of salt, mix in the egg and a little port. Stuff either turkey or chicken.

LAMB AND CHESTNUT PILAU

1 lb. lamb	Water
1 lb. chestnuts	Butter
½ lb. long grain rice	Salt and pepper

Wash and drain the rice. Boil and peel the chestnuts in the usual way and simmer the lamb in salted water until it is tender. Drain the meat, cut it into pieces and fry it in a little butter. Add the chestnuts with 3 cups of water, and bring it to the boil, adding the rice and seasoning. Simmer all this very slowly indeed for about ½ hour.

FRESHWATER FISH STUFFED WITH CHESTNUTS

3 lb. fish	1 tspn. salt
3 onions	¼ tspn. mace
2½ cups white wine	¼ tspn. thyme
6 tbsp. butter	¼ tspn. black pepper
Thick slice bread	¼ tspn. bay leaves
1 clove garlic	1 egg
12 chestnuts	Lemon juice
1 tbsp. parsley	Bread crumbs

Chop 1 onion and cook it until golden in 3 tablespoons butter. Add a thick slice of bread cut into squares which have been soaked in ½ cup of dry white wine, then squeezed dry. Add the parsley, 2 chopped onions, 1 clove garlic either pressed or chopped, salt, pepper, powdered mace, bay, thyme and the boiled and peeled chestnuts. Mix all this thoroughly and let it cool. Then add the egg to bind it all. Use this to stuff the head and cavity of the fish, and then tie the fish up carefully with skewers, etc. Let it stand for a couple of hours, so that the herbs impregnate the fish, then put it in an earthenware dish covered with 2 cups of dry white wine (preferably home-made), and add salt to taste. Cook in a moderate oven for 20 minutes. Baste it, and cover the fish with breadcrumbs and a squirt of lemon juice. Cook it for a further 20 minutes before serving.

BRAISED CHESTNUTS

Chestnuts	Bouquet garni with
Veal stock	celery
Knob of butter	Salt and pepper

Peel the chestnuts in the usual way, and put them in a flat buttered dish with a bouquet garni and lots of celery (wild celery will do very well indeed). Season well, and just cover the chestnuts in thick veal stock. Cover the dish and cook it in a slow to moderate oven for ¾ hour. Be careful not to break up the chestnuts too much when preparing them. They make a very good garnish when cooked this way.

CHESTNUT FLOUR DISHES
Polenta
Sieve some chestnut flour into lightly salted boiling water and mix it well. Continue cooking until it starts to dry out and no longer sticks to the side of the pan. Pour it on to a floured board and cut it into slices. These can be eaten with cheese (the Corsicans have goats' milk or ewes' milk cheese), or else grilled and fried.
Brilloli
A porridge is made with chestnut flour with extra milk or cream. If oil is put with this it becomes *Feriana*.
Tourte
This again is similar to Brilloli, but aniseed, pine kernels and dried raisins are added and the whole thing is cooked in the oven.
Castagnacci
These are simply thick fritters using chestnut flour instead of wheat flour, quickly fried and turned in very hot fat.

CHESTNUT MOUSSE

2 doz. chestnuts	Vanilla essence
½ pt. water	½ pt. cream
4 oz. sugar	Egg white

Boil the chestnuts, peel them and pound them to a paste. Put them in a saucepan with the water, sugar and a little vanilla essence. Boil this, stirring all the time until it is very smooth, then take it off the heat, and when cool, stir into it the whipped cream with the egg white beaten into it. Chill it thoroughly in the fridge before serving.

CHESTNUTS AND APPLE PUDDING

About 30 chestnuts	Sugar to taste
1 lb. apples	

Roast the chestnuts, remove the shells and skins and flatten them. Arrange them in a pie dish to line it. Meanwhile make a purée of the cooked apples and sugar and spread this over the chestnuts. Cook in a moderate oven for not more than $\frac{1}{2}$ hour with a cover on the dish. If it dries out, add a little syrup. Before serving, turn the dish upside down, so that the chestnut purée makes a crust on top.

CHESTNUT PUDDING

6 oz. peeled chestnuts	2 oz. butter
2 oz. sponge cake crumbs	4 eggs
	1 tbsp. rum
1 oz. chocolate or coffee flavouring	1 oz. caster sugar
	$\frac{1}{2}$ pt. milk
2 oz. flour	

Prepare the chestnuts, and cook them in a little water until they are tender. Rub them through a fine sieve, or put them through a blender. Break the chocolate into small pieces and melt it in the milk in a pan over a low heat (or add the coffee essence to the milk). In another pan melt the butter, stir in the flour, cook it for a minute then add the chocolate milk, stirring it until it boils. Add the cake crumbs and stir well. When the mixture has cooled, beat in the egg yolks, chestnut purée, and rum. Whisk the egg whites stiffly, fold them into the mixture, pour it all into a well-buttered dish, cover it with foil, and bake in a moderate oven for 1 hour. Serve it with cream.

MARRONS GLACÉE
Chestnuts
Strong syrup
  (see page 25)

Lemon juice
Icing sugar

Peel and boil some chestnuts in the usual way, being careful not to break them. Press them together in pairs. Dip each pair into the syrup and boil them for a few minutes. Coat them thickly with icing sugar, brown them in the oven and squeeze a little lemon juice over them. Chill them in the fridge before eating.

CHESTNUT CONFECTION
Shelled chestnuts
Equal amount of
  sugar

$\frac{1}{2}$ weight crab apple
  jelly

Shell the chestnuts then blanch them in boiling water and remove all the brown skin. Sieve them very finely, or put them through a blender. Weigh them and then clarify the same amount of sugar, cooked to ball (250°F. or 121°C.). Remove the syrup from the heat and mix in half its weight of crab apple jelly. Add the chestnuts and stir well. Spread this on to a flat baking tray, about $\frac{1}{4}$ inch thick, and put it into a very cool oven to dry. The following day, cut it into squares, put them on a sieve, and turn them occasionally until they are completely dry. Store those that are not eaten at once in airtight tins.

CHESTNUT JAM
2 lb. chestnuts
2 lb. sugar

6 tbsp. orange
  flower water
Vanilla essence

Skin and peel the chestnuts in the usual way. Boil them until they are tender, then drain them and cook them in the orange flower water with the sugar and a few drops of vanilla essence. Stir them until the mixture is quite soft. The preserve is ready when a little dropped in water, goes solid. Keep it in sealed jars.

CHICKWEED Fam. Caryophyllaceae

Stellaria media

Chick Wittles, Chicknyweed, Clucken Wort, Skirt Buttons, Star Chickweed

This must not be confused with the dark green, tough-looking, whiskery, mouse-ear chickweed that infests lawns. The edible star chickweed is smooth, and its translucent stems have only a single line of fine hairs that runs up to a joint, then stops, changes sides, to carry on to the next node.

The small white flowers have deeply cleft petals and hairy sepals with white margins. Chickweed grows everywhere, especially on ground that has been cultivated or dug, or otherwise disturbed, then left fallow.

BUTTERED CHICKWEED

Chickweed	Shallots, spring
Butter	onions or chives
Salt and pepper	Nutmeg
	Lemon juice

Chickweed shrinks rather when cooked, but is well worth while gathering as it tastes rather like the tenderest early spinach. Wash it and put it in a pan with a knob of butter, salt and pepper, and chopped chives, shallots, or spring onions, and a little nutmeg. Drain and serve it with a squeeze of lemon juice.

CHICKWEED SANDWICHES

Chickweed	Lemon juice
Salt and pepper	Worcester sauce

Add a little lemon juice, salt and pepper, and a few drops of Worcester sauce to the cress. Chickweed goes particularly well with tomato or any other sandwich filling that is improved by a bit of green.

CHICKWEED SALAD

Wash the plants well and shake them dry. Use your favourite dressing on the chickweed, which can be the main green in the salad, or added to lettuce, etc.

CHICORY Fam. Compositae

Chichorium intybus

This plant grows up to about 3 ft. high in pastures and grassy places, and prefers chalk and limestone soils. It is a stiff plant with tough stems and branches, rather sparsely clad with leaves growing in clusters from which spring the bright blue flowers like single dandelions. Lower down the stem are the large, rather irregularly shaped leaves which are best for salad.

The roots are cut into pieces, dried and reduced to a fine grain or powder to make coffee on the continent, but in this country the main culinary use for chicory is in salad. The leaves, and for a stronger flavour, the flowers, being eaten. Older leaves can be used boiled and buttered as a vegetable. Cook the roots as a vegetable as one does carrots.

'To make Conserve of Cichory flowers: Take of your Cicory flowers new gathered; for if you let them but an hour or two at the most, they will lose their colour, and do you very little service; therefore weigh them presently, and to every ounce of flowers you must take three ounces of double refined Sugar, and beat them together in a Mortar of Alabaster and a wooden Pestle, till such time as they bee thoroughly beaten; for, the better the Flowers and Sugar be beaten, the better will your conserve be; let this always be for a generall rule; and being well brayed, you must take them up, and put it into a Chaser cleane scoured, and set it on the fire till it be thoroughly hot: then take it off, and put it up, and keepe it all the yeare.'

Sir Hugh Plat, *A Closet for Ladies*, 1608.

CHIVES Fam. Liliaceae

Allium schoenoprasum

This plant grows 6 to 9 inches high and has greyish hollow leaves rather like rushes. The round head has dense purple-pink flowers and does not have the bulbils of wild garlic which it otherwise much resembles. Chives are used extensively for flavouring and for garnishing soups and salads, and are oniony but not so strong as garlic. They are also good chopped and combined with eggs or cream cheeses.

Chives are grown as a garden plant, but can be found as an escape.

See also: Chickweed (Buttered); Dandelion (Buttered) and (Pissenlit au Lard); Nettles (Creamed); Sow Thistle (Buttered); and Herb Mayonnaise (page 36); Herbed Eggs en Cocotte (page 205).

CLARY Fam. Labiatae

Salvia horminoides
Wild Sage

This plant likes dry grassy places and is more common in the south than in the north. It grows up to 3 ft. high and has greyish jaggedly toothed leaves. The flowers are mauvish-white and compact, growing round the stem in sets so that the effect is finally a spike of flowers.

Clary flowers are used chopped in omelettes, or dipped in sweet batter and fried, eaten with sugar and lemon juice like pancakes.

CLARY WINE

3 pts. clary flowers
2½ lb. sugar
Handful raisins
2 lemons

1 gal. water
½ tspn. yeast nutrient
¾ oz. yeast

Make a syrup with the sugar and water. Put the blossoms, raisins, and lemon rind (without white pith) into a container and pour the syrup over them. Stir well, and when cool add the yeast. Cover the container and leave it for 4 days. Then strain the contents into a fermentation jar, add the yeast nutrient and lemon juice, ferment to a finish, rack, mature and bottle.

Or pour boiling water over the blossoms and raisins, stir well, and after 2 days strain into a fermentation jar and add the sugar made into a syrup, the lemon juice, yeast nutrient, and yeast. Ferment to a finish, rack, mature and bottle. This makes a much lighter wine.

CLOVER Fam. Papilionaceae

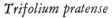

Trifolium pratense   *T. repens*

These are the two most common red and white clovers, but there are many other varieties, and because specially produced strains of clover are sown everywhere as parts of seed mixtures in grassland farming, many of the species which abound are in fact escapes. These can all be used. Clovers are typified by their familiar trefoil leaves. They have dense globular heads, and if you pull out the petals, and suck the bases, you can taste the honey.

CLOVER TEA
Pour 1 pt. of boiling water over 1 oz. of the plant, both flowers and leaves.

CLOVER WINE

1 gal. clover flowers	3 lemons
1 gal. water	2 oranges
3 lb. white sugar	1 oz. yeast

Put the flowers and the thin peel of the oranges and lemons (without the pith) into a container, and pour boiling water over them. Leave for 2 days, then strain off the liquid and make a syrup with it. Add the fruit juices and yeast, and put it all into a fermentation jar. Ferment to a finish.

Another method is to pour the boiling water over the clover flowers and when it is lukewarm add all the other ingredients, and let it stand covered for 4 days before straining and bottling.

COLTSFOOT Fam. Compositae

Foalfoot, Coughweed

Tussilago Farfara

Coltsfoot flowers open in early spring before the leaves appear. It has leafless stems, purple with a whitish woolly appearance, covered in scales which overlap each other. The flowers are yellow, rather like small dandelions, but do not open so fully. The leaves are big with fine black teeth, heart-shaped, and downy when they first appear, becoming green later. Coltsfoot is common on bare ground, particularly on clay, but does not grow in any thick grass or other vegetation. Coltsfoot has always been used as a cough cure, in fact chemists' shops in

France bear a picture of the coltsfoot as a kind of trade sign. It has also been used as a substitute for tobacco, and is usually an ingredient of herbal smoking mixtures.

COLTSFOOT WINE

1 gal. coltsfoot flowers	1 lemon
1 gal. water	3½ lb. white sugar
3 oranges	1 oz. yeast

Put the flowers into a container with the other ingredients excepting the yeast, sugar until it is dissolved and then pour it over the flowers, etc. Allow the mixture to cool and add the yeast. Cover it and allow it to stand for 4 days before straining the liquid through a coarse strainer into the fermentation jar. Ferment to a finish, rack, mature and bottle.

CORIANDER Fam. Umbelliferae

Coriandrum sativum

'And the house of Israel called the name thereof Manna, and it was like coriander seed, white; and the taste of it was like wafers made with honey.'　　　　*Exodus* xvi, 31.

A casual and local escape in this country. It stands from 4 to 10 in. high and has an unpleasant smell. The umbel flowers are pinkish and grow on solid stems. The lower leaves grow opposite each other and are broad, while the upper leaves are long and narrow. The seeds are used as a cooking herb, and appear in the round ridged red-brown fruits which are about ⅛ to ¼ in. in diameter. The seeds are light yellow, have an aromatic smell of sandalwood, and a taste which is both sweet and bitter, rather like burnt orange peel. They are used to flavour a large variety of food, meat, cheese, pickle, salads, puddings and pastries.

However, this herb is not used half as much these days as it once was, especially in sweet dishes, as flavouring for custard and milk puddings, cakes and biscuits, apple pie, and even on junket. For all these uses the seeds must be bruised or ground.

Crushed with garlic they improve pork or mutton. Use a teaspoonful of each, and stuff the mixture into slits in the meat.

A few coriander seeds can be added to stews or casseroles, especially those made from pork. Coriander is also a very important ingredient of curry powder, and in fact can be added to any spiced dish. When making vinegar pickles, a few coriander seeds added (with other herbs) to the vinegar when it is boiled, improve its flavour, and chutneys can always have coriander as a flavouring ingredient.

CORIANDER CORDIAL

1 oz. coriander seed	1 pt. brandy
¼ oz. caraway seed	1 pt. strong syrup
Piece of cinnamon	(see page 25)

Steep the spices in the brandy for 3 weeks. strain off and add to the syrup. Stir well and bottle.
See also: Highland Bitters (page 208); Vespetro (page 208).

COWSLIP Fam. Primulaceae

'The Use of Conserve of Cowslips: That of Cowslips doth marvelously strengthen the Braine, preserveth against Madnesse, against the decay of memory, stoppeth Head-ache and most infirmities thereof.'
A Book of Fruit and Flowers, 1653.

Cowslips are perhaps less common than they once were, but still very common in the south, mostly in grassland, on chalk,

D

Primula veris

limestone or clay. They flower in April and May, and have a
most characteristic and unmistakable beautiful honey smell.
The flowers grow in umbels on the top of long bare stems,
and are like small drooping primroses with long pale green
calyxes. The leaves are like small primrose leaves, narrow at
the base and rather fleshy.

The flower heads can be eaten, a few at a time, with salads.

PICKLED COWSLIPS

1 lb. cowslips	1 pt. white wine
1 lb. white sugar	vinegar

Make sure that the cowslip heads are clean. Boil the white
wine vinegar and sugar to a syrup. Add the cowslips, and when
they are well mixed, bottle and seal in the usual way.

COWSLIP PUDDING

2 qts. cowslips	4 eggs
2 oz. finely crushed	Rose water
biscuits or bread	Sugar
¾ pt. milk	Butter

Remove the stalks and seeds from the cowslip heads. Cut them
up finely and pound them. Add the crushed biscuits or bread
and the milk. Bring them to the boil, then when it is cool,
add the eggs, well beaten, and a little rose water added to

them. Sweeten the whole lot to taste, pour it into a buttered dish and bake it in a very slow oven in a bain marie until set. Sprinkle a little caster sugar over the top before serving.

COWSLIP CREAM

3 handfuls cowslips
1 qt. cream
Pinch mace

Castor sugar to
taste
2 tspn. orange juice
2 egg yolks

Bruise 2 handfuls of cowslips. Bring them just to the boil in the cream using a double saucepan. Add the mace, orange juice and sugar, and stir well. Strain the mixture to remove the bits and pour it back into the saucepan. Beat the egg yolks lightly and add them to the mixture. Reheat, stirring all the time until it thickens. Do not let it boil or it will curdle. Put the mixture into the fridge until it is chilled, and before serving, garnish it with the rest of the flowers or with candied cowslips. (Cowslip flowers are candied in exactly the same way as are violets. See the recipe for crystallised violets on page 194.)

COWSLIP WINE

1 gal. cowslips,
   yellow petals
1 gal. water
2 oranges

2 lemons
3 lb. sugar
1 Campden tablet
$\frac{3}{4}$ oz. yeast

This makes a light summery wine, fairly sweet. Put the flowers and the thinly peeled rinds of the citrus fruit (without white pith) and the Campden tablet into a container and pour the boiling water over them. Cover and leave for 2 days, stirring several times. Strain off the juice, and when the liquid is cool, add the yeast. Pour into fermentation jars. Ferment to a finish, rack, mature and bottle.

COWSLIP MEAD

1 gal. cowslip heads
1 gal. water
2 lb. honey

1 lemon
2 sprigs sweet briar
$\frac{1}{2}$ oz. yeast

Boil the honey and the water together for an hour, skimming well. Put 1 pint of liquor in a jug with the thinly peeled rind of the lemon and its juice. Pour the remainder of the syrup over the cowslip heads, and leave covered for 48 hours. Then strain into fermentation jars with the lemon liquor, sweet briar and yeast. Continue as usual.

CRAB APPLE Fam. Rosaceae

Malus sylvestris

Crab apple is the wild apple stock on which all cultivated apples are grown and from which they have been developed. The true tree is small, deciduous, with pointed oval leaves and red-brown twigs. The flowers, like cultivated apple blossom, are pinkish white with yellow stamens and grow in clusters. Many wild apple trees in our hedgerows are not true crab apple, but have grown from cultivated apple seeds thrown away in cores, or carried there by birds. Crab apples are small and usually much more sour than cultivated apples, and are yellowish green, sometimes ripening to scarlet. The fruit, like all apples, contains plenty of pectin, so it's a good 'setter' and is often added to other fruits for this quality.

Recipes containing crab apples usually need a little extra sweetening, and as sure as God made little green apples, if anyone eats too many of them raw, the effects will be drastic!

CRAB APPLE AND WILD CELERY CURRY

1½ lb. crab apples	½ pt. tomato juice
1½ lb. cooking apples	4 tbsp. butter
8 oz. diced celery	⅛ tspn. cayenne
4 oz. raisins	pepper
1 tbsp. curry powder	Salt

Wash and chop the apples and brown them in the butter. Take them out of the pan and in it fry the curry powder and cayenne to dark brown. It will take about 3 minutes. Put the apples back in the pan with all the other ingredients. Cover them and simmer for about 30 minutes, or until the celery is tender, and the mixture fairly dry. Serve it on boiled rice.

CRAB APPLE PICKLE

5 or 6 lb. crab apples	Spices (ginger,
3 lb. sugar	cinnamon, cloves
1 qt. vinegar	of garlic, etc.)

Wash and dry the crab apples, just removing the stalk and blossom end. Make a syrup with the vinegar and sugar, and when it is dissolved add a little crushed ginger, cinnamon, and a few cloves of garlic in a muslin bag. Put the apples in the syrup, making sure that they are covered by it, and heat them gently until they are tender, but not burst. Strain the crab apples out and put them in a jar, cooking the rest of the apples until they are all cooked. Reduce the syrup, and pour it over them, and seal the jars in the usual way.

CRAB APPLE PUDDING

Crab apples	Lemon juice
Sugar	Gelatine

Cut the fruit in half, and put it in a pan with enough cold water to cover it. Simmer it gently until tender, then strain it. Replace the liquid in the pan. To each pint allow 1 lb. sugar and 1 dspn. lemon juice. Simmer this gently for 1 hour and skim. Measure the liquid again and to each pint allow ½ oz. gelatine dissolved in a little warm water, and add this to the liquid in the pan. Stir it well then pour it all into a mould and put it in the fridge to set.

CRAB APPLE JELLY

6 lb. crab apples	5 pts. water
5 lb. sugar	1 lemon

Wash and halve the crab apples and put them in a pan with the water. Cook them until they are soft and then leave them to drip in a bag overnight. About 5 pints of juice should be extracted, and to this add the same amount of sugar and the juice of a large lemon. Boil this for about 20 minutes, stirring well, then skim it, and put it into jars and seal in the usual way.

CRAB APPLE WINE

1 gal. sliced crab	Pectozyme
apples	½ tspn. yeast nutrient
1 gal. water	¾ oz. yeast
3 lb. demerara sugar	

Put the apples in a container and pour *cold* water over them, and sprinkle in the pectozyme. Leave this covered for 3 days, stirring frequently, then strain and squeeze out the juice. Add the sugar, and stir well until it is dissolved. Add the nutrient and yeast, put it all into fermentation jars, ferment to a finish, rack, mature and bottle.

This method and recipe differs from that used for wine made from almost every other fruit or flower, as cold water is used. This is because the fruit contains so much pectin which boiling water would release into the must. The resultant wine would be very hard indeed to clear.

To make a heavier wine, add ½ lb. raisins with the sugar.

See also: Blackberry (and Crab Apple Pudding); Elderberry (and Crab Apple Jelly); Chestnut (Confection).

CRANBERRY Fam. Ericaceae

Cranberries are quite common, but tend to be local as they grow in bogs, particularly where sphagnum moss abounds. It is a low creeping shrub with a few oval, dark green leaves, with margins rolled downwards. The four-petalled flowers are bright pink and the fruit are small whitish berries, spotted with red.

Vaccinium oxycoccus
Mossberry

CRANBERRY PRESERVE

Cover the cranberries with water, boil for 10 to 15 minutes and put the purée in large covered jars. Use it for any recipe, at your convenience. A drink made from this, sweetened to taste and diluted with water, is very refreshing.

CRANBERRY TART

1 qt. cranberries	Pastry
1 lb. stoned raisins	Vanilla essence
Sugar	Milk

Clean the cranberries, and arrange them in layers with the raisins, each sprinkled with sugar. Leave them for some hours to let the sugar and juice mix. Then put the fruit in a pan (don't add water), and simmer for about 5 minutes. Line a dish with pastry, either flaky or short crust, and add the fruit mixture. Cover it with more pastry, glaze with a little milk, and bake it in a hot oven until the pastry is golden.

CRANBERRY CHEESE

1 pt. cranberries	2 oz. chopped raisins
½ pt. water	2 oz. chopped walnuts
¾ lb. sugar	1 orange

Cook the cranberries until they are soft, in the water. Put them through a sieve and add to this purée the sugar, raisins, and walnuts. Cook this until it boils, stirring all the time, then add a very thinly sliced orange. Simmer this for 20 minutes, pour it into pots, and serve it cold.

CRANBERRY JELLY

Cranberries   Sugar
Water

Cover the berries with water and cook them for about 15 minutes. Add 1¼ cups of sugar for each 1 lb. of fruit, and cook again until it is a thick syrup, which sets when tested. Put it in jars and seal.

CRANBERRY SAUCE

1 lb. cranberries   Teacupful water
¼ lb. sugar   Port

Pick and wash the cranberries. Simmer them in the water until they are reduced to a pulp. Add the sugar and a little port. Serve with turkey.

CRANBERRY WINE

1 gal. cranberries   1 lb. raisins
3 lb. sugar   ¾ oz. yeast
1 gal. water

Pour boiling water over the cranberries, mash the mixture well for 3 days, then strain it. Add the raisins, the sugar made into a syrup, and when cool, add the yeast. Put it into fermentation jars, ferment to a finish, rack, mature and bottle.

See also: Strawberry (Wild-Cottage Cheese with Strawberries) which can be made with Cranberries.

CURRANTS Fam. Grossulariaceae

Although we know these as common garden fruit bushes they all do grow wild, especially near water. There are many wild blackcurrant bushes in the Norfolk Broads area, and elsewhere in East Anglia, and in fact they can be found all over Britain. In many cases they are escapes from cultivation, but where they have become established they form enormous thickets of fruiting bushes. They do not fruit well every year, but can yield fine crops. They are unfortunately subject to the same diseases

Ribes rubrum
Redcurrant
Ribes rubrum
Whitecurrant

Ribes nigrum
Blackcurrant

as cultivated varieties and sometimes get hard hit by them. They are all well enough known to need no botanical descriptions. The leaves of the blackcurrant are sticky and aromatic whereas the leaves of the other two have little smell.

Fruit syrups can be made out of any of these fruits. Blackcurrant especially is full of Vitamin C and is a splendid fruit. It is excellent for wine making, producing wonderfully coloured, full flavoured wines, with very little trouble. It is second only to elderberry as a wine making fruit.

SUMMER PUDDING
1 lb. blackcurrants	Sugar
$\frac{1}{2}$ lb. redcurrants	Cream
$\frac{1}{2}$ lb. raspberries	Kirsch or
$\frac{1}{2}$ lb. strawberries	cherry brandy
Loaf of white bread	

Stew all the fruit together until it is cooked but not mushy. Add enough sugar to make it really sweet and cook it for a few minutes longer. Line a pudding basin with medium thick slices of white bread, with the crusts removed, half fill the basin with fruit, then put in more slices of bread, making sure that they are completely saturated in the fruit. Continue the layers until the pudding is solid and soggy. Put a saucer on top and press it down until the juice begins to run out. Put the pudding in the fridge and leave it for 24 hours. It should be very cold but not frozen. Turn it out on to a plate and pour all the remaining fruit over it. If you have made it properly it should keep its shape. Serve it with absolutely masses and masses of cream.

The quantities and varieties of fruit used can be varied according to what is available, but blackcurrants are essential. To improve it even further, add some kirsch or cherry brandy to the fruit after it has been stewed, and put some more in the cream.

CURRANT PUDDING

Red, white or black   Sugar
　　currants   Suet pastry

Stew the currants in very little water with sugar to taste, then put a layer of them in a greased pudding basin, then a layer of suet pastry. Repeat this until the basin is almost full, cover it with greaseproof paper, and steam it for 2 hours.

BLACKCURRANT LEAF CREAM

1 cupful young black-   2 egg whites
　　currant leaves   Lemon juice
1 lb. sugar $\frac{1}{4}$ pt. whipped cream
$\frac{1}{2}$ pt. water

Boil the sugar, water and blackcurrant leaves without stirring for 15 minutes. Strain them and pour the cooled syrup very gently on to the beaten egg whites. Beat this all the time until it begins to thicken. Stir in the lemon juice and whipped cream. Cool it thoroughly in the fridge before serving.

REDCURRANT COMPÔTE

1 lb. redcurrants   2 tbsp. water
7 oz. sugar

Stalk the ripe redcurrants and wash them in cold water without letting them soak. Put them in a pan with the sugar and water. Shake them over a low flame until the sugar has dissolved, then put them in the fridge in a serving bowl. Leave them for 3 hours, by which time they should have formed a red jelly. Serve them with whipped cream.

BLACKCURRANT AND APPLE JELLY

4 lb. blackcurrants	1 lb. sugar to 1 pint
2 lb. apples	of fruit juice
3 pts. water	Lemon juice

Clean and pick the blackcurrants and peel and core the apples. Put them both in a pan with the water and simmer them until the juice is extracted and the apples are soft. Drain them through a bag, and to each pint of juice add 1 lb. of sugar, and the juice of $\frac{1}{2}$ a lemon. Boil this for $\frac{1}{2}$ hour, put the jelly into jars, and seal them as usual.

BLACKCURRANT WINE

3 lb. fruit	1 lemon
1 gal. water	$\frac{1}{4}$ pt. cold tea
3 lb. sugar	$\frac{3}{4}$ oz. yeast
$\frac{1}{2}$ tspn. yeast nutrient	

Put the fruit into a container and pour enough water over it to cover it. Mash it well and leave it to stand for 2 days, stirring frequently. Strain off the liquid, and make syrup with the sugar and enough water to make up the gallon. Add this to the juice with the cold tea and the juice of the lemon, and when it is cool, add the yeast and nutrient, and put the lot into a fermentation jar. Ferment to a finish, rack, mature and bottle.

To make a drier wine, reduce the amount of sugar to 2 lb. To make a heavier port type wine, add a $\frac{1}{4}$ lb. raisins to the must, omit the yeast nutrient, and use a port wine yeast.
See also: Bilberry (Red Currant Jelly); Cherry (Wild-Jam); Laver (Sauce 2); Nettle (Beer 2); Nettle (Country Pudding).

DANDELION Fam. Compositae

Surely too well known to need a description, this plant as a herbal medicine has a diuretic effect; hence its descriptive French name of Pissenlit!

Taraxacum officinale

In old kitchen gardens rows of dandelions were bred up to a huge size, some blanched like chicory. The leaves, shredded or chopped, roots and the flowers were all used in salads. In France today, dandelions are sold in markets. The young leaves are usually mixed with other vegetables to vary the flavours.

PISSENLIT AU LARD

Pickled pork or bacon	Vinegar
Fat for frying	Olive oil
Dandelion	Salt and pepper

Trim blanched pickled pork or bacon cut into small pieces, fry them until crisp and dry, and serve them on a raw dandelion salad with a dressing of vinegar and olive oil, seasoned with salt and pepper.

Extra garnish can be added to the dandelion salad by adding finely chopped chives, parsley, garlic or borage. It can be eaten as a side dish with any rich meat.

BUTTERED DANDELION

Dandelion leaves	Lemon juice
Butter	Chopped chives or
Salt and pepper	parsley

Wash young dandelion leaves and put them still slightly wet in a pan. Add a lump of butter, salt and pepper to taste, then cook them slowly until tender. Keep stirring to prevent them sticking to the pan. Strain and add a squeeze of lemon juice and garnish with chopped chives or parsley.

DANDELION SALAD

Dandelion leaves	Salted water
Olive oil	Lemon juice

Boil the young dandelion leaves very quickly in plenty of salted water until they are tender, then drain them, and serve them cold with an olive oil and lemon juice dressing.

DANDELION PURÉE

Dandelion leaves	Flour
Butter	Bread
Milk	Salt and pepper

Pick plenty of young dandelion leaves, wash them well and boil them in salted water. Drain them carefully, and put them through a sieve. Make a thick roux with the butter, flour and a little milk, add the dandelion purée, and season it to taste with salt and pepper. Heat it well and serve it with fried bread.

DANDELION COFFEE

Dandelion coffee tastes like weak coffee, but has no caffeine and is therefore easily digested and makes a good drink.

Clean the roots and dry them thoroughly. Roast them to coffee colour in a cool oven, store (for a short time only) in an airtight tin or jar, and grind them when needed. Make the coffee with boiling water and add milk and sugar to taste.

DANDELION BEER

$\frac{1}{2}$ lb. dandelion plants	$\frac{1}{2}$ oz. root ginger
1 gal. water	1 oz. cream of tartar
1 lb. Demerara sugar	1 oz. yeast
1 lemon	

Pull up the whole of the dandelion plant in springtime when the flowers are just blooming. Wash the plants and remove the hairs from the main tap root. Boil them together with the bruised ginger and the lemon rind (without white pith) for 10 minutes. Strain out the solids and pour the liquid over the sugar and cream of tartar in a fermentation jar, stirring until the sugar has dissolved. When it is lukewarm add the lemon juice and yeast, cover the jar and leave it in a warm place for

3 days. Strain it again and bottle in screwtopped cider or beer bottles, which should be stored on their sides. The beer is ready to drink in about a week, and should hiss when the stopper is loosened. Dandelion beer does not keep for very long.

DANDELION WINE 1 (Dry and Light)

3 qts. dandelion petals	2 lemons
2½ lb. white sugar	1 gal. water
2 oranges	¾ oz. yeast

Use only the yellow petals as the rest of the plant is bitter. Put them in a container and steep them in boiling water, leaving them for 2 days. Make a syrup with the sugar and add it with the other ingredients; thinly peeled fruit rinds, juice (and raisins and ginger in Recipe 2) to the strained juice from the flowers. When the liquid is cool, add the yeast, and leave it to ferment for 3 days before straining it into fermentation jars.

DANDELION WINE 2 (Sweet and Heavier)

3 quarts petals	½ lb. raisins
3½ lb. demerara sugar	½ oz. root ginger
1 lemon	¾ oz. yeast
1 orange	1 gal. water

If you wish to make a heavier more gingery wine, put the rinds, raisins and ginger into the fermentation jar with the liquids. Add the yeast, ferment to a finish, rack, mature and bottle.

DULSE Fam. Rhodophyceae

Rhodymenia palmata

A red seaweed which grows to about 15 in. long. It has fairly wide, flat-lobed fronds. It grows near low tide level, often attached to the stalks of the seaweed Laminaria, which is that familiar big strap of brownish leathery weed with one big thick stalk ending in a branching root.

Wash the dulse and simmer it in water until it is tender. Strain it, cut it into small pieces and put it into a pan with a knob of butter, and reheat it. Season it with salt and pepper.

Dulse can also be eaten raw, boiled, or cooked over embers, or rolled on a flat stone with a red-hot poker until it turns green. It can also be dried and eaten as a savory or relish with potatoes.

A jelly can be made by letting the dulse simmer in milk until it is dissolved, then set aside to cool. See Carrageen Mould (page 75).

See also: Laver (Seaweed Soup – which can be made with Dulse instead of Laver).

ELDER Fam. Caprifoliaceae

Sambucus nigra

Elder is an extremely common hedgerow bush growing 10–12 ft. high. In May/June it carries masses of flowers in creamy clusters with a characteristic rather sickly muscatel smell. These later turn to rich deep, red/black berries hanging in clusters almost as big as your hand. Elderflowers and berries are much used on the continent, but neglected in England. Used as flavouring the flowers are fine, but the berries, if stewed by themselves, are a little strong and bitter, although sugar improves them. Elder makes a good fruit jelly preserve, and both flowers and berries make wine. In fact elder is probably the best and most easily obtained wine ingredient we have growing wild in this country. Some call it the English grape, and hate to see it ignored or treated as a weed. Elderflower and elderberry wine, properly made, can stand with any wine for flavour and colour, and a beginner at winemaking can do no better than make a start on elder.

The elder tree is usually found near homes because in olden days it was planted as a protection from evil spirits. The tree itself was a protection, for the Norse mother of the good fairies, Hulda, lived under its roots, and this is where the name comes from. The superstition probably came with the Danes, and right up to the Middle Ages, the elder tree was held in great respect. It was the custom to make crosses with elderberry juice on the hearthstone to ward off witches and warlocks. To this day, in some parts of northern Europe, it is wise to ask permission of a village 'elder' before cutting it down.

BUTTERED ELDER STALKS

1 lb. green elder stalks	$\frac{1}{2}$ cup water
2 tbsp. butter	Salt
Juice $\frac{1}{4}$ lemon	

Pare away the woody outer casing, then cook the green elder stalks in the same way as artichoke stalks or chichory.

Put 1 lb. of stalks in a saucepan with the butter, pinch of salt, lemon juice and water. Bring them to boil, and simmer them for 45 minutes.

Or use 3 tablespoons of butter to cook them in, and don't use any water.

ELDERFLOWER FLAVOURING

Elderflowers add a distinctive flavour to milk dishes, jellies, gooseberry jam, or gooseberry or apple tarts. Tie the flowers in a muslin bag, boil or bake them with the dish, but remove them before serving.

ELDERBERRY SOUP

1 lb. elderberries	3½ oz. sugar
1¾ pts. water	¾ oz. cornflour
Lemon rind and juice	

Wash the fruit well and strip it from the stalks. Put it in a pan with the water, add a little lemon rind and simmer it until tender. Rub the berries through a fine sieve, or put it through a blender, and bring them to the boil again. Blend the cornflour with a little water, add it to the purée, and stir it all the time until completely cooked. Season with lemon juice and sugar, and serve the soup either hot or cold with croutons of fried bread.

ELDERBERRY CHUTNEY

2 lb. elderberries	½ tspn. ground ginger
½ pt. vinegar	½ tspn. cayenne pepper
¼ pt. chilli vinegar	½ tspn. mustard
¼ lb. chopped onion	½ tspn. cinnamon
¼ lb. seedless raisins	Grated nutmeg
3 oz. brown sugar	1 tspn. salt

Remove the stalks from the berries. Put the berries in a sauce-pan with the vinegars and mash them. Put the raisins and onions through a mincer and add them to the berries with the sugar and spices. Simmer them all together until thick, and season it to taste with salt and cayenne pepper. Pour it into warm jars, and seal them.

ELDERFLOWERS IN BATTER

Elderflower heads	2 eggs
Honey	1¾ cup milk
Lemon Juice	2 tbsp. oil
Batter 1.	*Batter 2.*
½ cup soy flour	2 eggs
1½ cups wholewheat flour	½ tspn. salt
	1–1¼ cups soy flour
2 tsp. brown sugar	1 cup milk
½ tspn salt	

Pick large flat elderflower heads, and strip off the florets and put as many as you like into the batter mixture. (The first batter mixture needs to be quite thin, as the wholemeal flour is self-raising.) Mix the florets well into the batter, and fry them in hot fat in the usual way, and serve the pancakes with honey and lemon juice to taste.

ELDERBERRY AND BLACKBERRY JAM

Elderberries   Sugar
Blackberries

Bruise the fruit slightly and bring it slowly to the boil and simmer for 20 minutes. Use ¾ lb. of sugar to each 1 lb. of fruit. Add it and boil again for 20 minutes. Skim well, put it into jars and seal them.

ELDERBERRY AND CRAB APPLE JELLY

2 qts. elderberries   2 pts. water
3 lb. crab apples   Rind of 1 orange
1 lb. sugar to each   1 tspn. cinnamon
   pt. juice

Chop the washed apples and stalk the elderberries before putting them into a preserving pan with the water. Simmer them gently until they are soft, then put them into a bag and leave it to drip overnight. Measure the juice, and add the sugar and boil them together until the jelly sets. Put it into jars and seal them.

ELDERBERRY SYRUP

2 qts. elderberries   12 cloves to each
1 lb. sugar to each   quart juice
   quart juice

Put 2 qts. of berries into a fireproof dish in a warm oven. Pour off the juice as it is released, and finally squeeze the juice out of the fruit and strain it into the rest. Add the sugar and cloves and simmer them for ½ hour. Strain, cork and bottle tightly. Use the syrup as a cough or sore throat mixture, or dilute it with hot water as a bed-time drink.

ELDERFLOWER DRINK

Dried flowers make a blossom flavoured tisane. Use 1 tea-spoonful of elderflowers per cup. Do not let it stand for longer than 3 or 4 minutes, strain it and sweeten it with honey.

Or: Fill a jug with fresh elderflowers, add boiling water, sweeten it to taste, and leave it to get cold, then strain it carefully before serving.

Or : Just pour cold water over half a jugful of fresh blossom, and leave it to stand for an hour.

ELDERBERRY DRINK

$\frac{1}{2}$ pt. elderberry juice

1$\frac{3}{4}$ pts. water

Lemon juice

Sugar

Mix the juice with water, season with lemon juice to taste, or put a slice of lemon in each glass when serving. Or liven it up with soda water. Sweeten to taste.

ELDERBERRY WINE

4 lb. elderberries

2$\frac{1}{2}$ lb. white sugar

1 gal. water

1 tbsp. cold tea

Juice of 1 lemon

$\frac{1}{2}$ tspn. yeast nutrient

1 Campden tablet

$\frac{3}{4}$ oz. yeast

Put the berries and Campden tablet in a container and pour $\frac{2}{3}$ gal. boiling water over them. Mash them well and leave covered for 2 days, mashing and stirring 2 or 3 times. Strain and squeeze off all the juice. Make up syrup with the rest of the water and the sugar, and when cool put it and all the other ingredients into a fermentation jar. Continue as usual.

This makes a medium dry wine. Increase sugar quantities to make a sweeter wine, use demarara sugar, $\frac{1}{2}$ lb. raisins and port-type yeast to make port. Reduce the quantities of elder-berries to produce a rose type wine. Experimentation will teach you that many types of red wine can be produced on an elderberry base.

ELDERFLOWER WINE

3 pts. elderflowers	$\frac{1}{2}$ tspn. yeast nutrient
1 gal. water	$\frac{3}{4}$ oz. g.p. yeast (or
2$\frac{1}{2}$ lb. sugar	champagne or white
Juice of 2 lemons	wine yeast)
1 tbsp. cold tea	

Put the flowers into a container and pour $\frac{2}{3}$ gal. of boiling water over them. Stir, and leave covered for 2 days. Strain the juice into a fermentation jar and add the other ingredients, making the sugar into a syrup with the rest of the water, and adding the yeast when the liquid has cooled. Ferment to a finish, rack, mature and bottle. This will make a well-flavoured wine. If you prefer a white wine with less blossom flavour, reduce the quantity of elderflowers. Adding $\frac{1}{4}$ lb. raisins, more sugar and the yellow rind as well as the juice of lemons and oranges, will produce a much richer, heavier, sweeter white wine.

Elderflower wine will often be found to be sparkling when opened. For some reason a slight fermentation seems to continue long after it has apparently ceased, and sometimes the wine will start a secondary fermentation in its bottles as spring and flowering time comes round again. Whatever the reasons, there is no more pleasant country white wine than sparkling elderflower.

FAT HEN Fam. Chenopodiaceae
Bacon Weed, Dirty Dick, Muck Hill, Midden Myles, Dung Weed, Melgs, All Good, Goose Foot, Pig Weed.

This is a very common plant indeed and is a real 'nuisance' weed. It grows up to 3 ft. high on red-streaked stems. The lower leaves are toothed and the leaves are generally the shape of a goose's foot, hence one of the many popular names. The flowers are in spikes at the end of the stems and in the angles between, and the leaves are whitish-green. The plant is generally mealy-looking. It likes rich soil and is often found growing round dung heaps.

Young seedlings are good in salads, and the tips of the older plants can be taken before they seed. In times past the seeds of fat hen were harvested to be dried and ground into

Chenopodium album

flour for making bread, cakes or gruel, as they still are in parts of America. They taste like buckwheat, and can be eaten raw.

BUTTERED FAT HEN

Young fat hen leaves   Nutmeg
1 tbsp. water   Knob of butter
Salt and pepper

Wash the leaves and small stalks and put them still dripping in the pan, with an extra spoonful of water to stop them burning. Cook them slowly, and keep turning them over. Drain when tender, and press out the water. Chop them finely, and re-heat them with salt, pepper, nutmeg and a lump of butter. Stir well and serve very hot.

FAT HEN SOUP

Handful young leaves   Nutmeg
1 pt. water   Pepper
Salt   Butter
1 tbsp. ground rice   Egg yolk
Milk   Cream

Wash the leaves and small stalks and put them in a pan with the cold water, salt and ground rice. Cook them with the lid

on until the greens are tender, then strain into a basin and rub
the solids through a sieve. Thin this down with the liquid
and some milk, add nutmeg and pepper and butter. Heat it
again, beating all the time, but do not let it boil. Add a little
cream, pour the soup into a tureen containing the beaten egg
yolk, with a little of the cooking liquid.

Add some shallots or onion (not too many) that have been
fried in butter for extra taste.

FENNEL Fam. Umbelliferae

Foeniculum vulgare

Fennel grows up to 6 ft. high, and it has bright yellow flowers
growing in umbels. The leaves are very feathery indeed with
sheaths at the bases. The stems are shiny, and become hollow
as the plant matures. The fruits which contain the seeds, are
narrow and ribbed. The plant can be found as an escape by
the sea and sometimes inland on waste ground. Although quite
common it is unrecognised by most as the source of the
familiar fennel seed, and the leaves and root are also quite
edible. The wild variety may not have such a strong flavour
and smell of aniseed as do some specially cultivated varieties.
The bulbous fennel root which is such a wonderful vegetable
is specially cultivated 'Florence fennel', difficult to grow well
in this country and never found wild here. Fennel has an
affinity with fish for which it is used as flavouring. It also

goes well with pork, veal and in salads. It is supposed to be slimming, and a few fennel seeds sprinkled in a salad do add an unusual flavour, and if taken daily, may help to keep down weight. It is also a digestive aid.

A few fennel seeds sprinkled in apple pie give it an unusual flavour.

Fennel can be added to salad dressing for beetroot or carrot. Or just chop it and add it to any green salad.

Add the flowers and semi-ripe seeds when pickling cucumbers and making sauerkraut.

FENNEL AND CUCUMBER SALAD

½ lb. fennel root and finely shredded lower stems	1 tbsp. lemon juice
	2 tbsp. olive oil
	Chopped parsley or chives
4 oz. cucumber	
6–8 radishes	Salt and pepper
½ tspn. chopped mint	

Cut out any discoloured or stringy bits of fennel. Wash and dry it and the radishes. Cut both into fine slices, and the cucumber into small chunks. Put them all in a bowl. Beat the lemon juice and oil together, season with salt and pepper, pour it over the vegetables, and stir well. Sprinkle with chopped parsley or chives before serving.

FENNEL SAUCE

2 tbsp. chopped fennel	¾ oz. flour
½ pt. water	Salt and pepper
1 oz. butter	

Melt the butter and stir in the flour and cook it for 2 or 3 minutes. Add the water, which should be hot but not boiling, and stir it in carefully. Bring it to the boil for a few minutes, and season it with salt and pepper and the fennel which has been previously boiled until tender. The sauce will have more flavour, if the water used is that in which the fennel pieces were previously cooked. Eat the sauce with fish, lamb, poultry or game.

FISH GRILLED WITH FENNEL

Fish	Butter
Fennel	Lemon juice
Salt	

Any whole fish, mackerel, herring, etc., can be used. Scale the fish, and gut it, and make 3 slits in each side of the body. Fill these and the cavity with fresh fennel, or dried seeds, and salt. Melt some butter and lemon juice in a grill pan, coat the fish thoroughly with it and grill it for a few minutes on each side.

FRESHWATER FISH WITH FLAMING FENNEL

Any 3 lb. freshwater fish; trout, red mullet, or sea bass.	Salt and pepper
	1 qt. fennel greens
	Butter
2 tbsp. brandy	

Wash, clean and completely dry the fish. Rub it with salt and pepper inside, and paint it all over with melted butter. Put it under the grill for 25 minutes, turning the fish twice and basting it with butter each time. Wash and dry the fennel greens carefully, and when the fish is cooked, put it on a hot stainless steel dish. Pour $\frac{1}{2}$ cup melted butter over the fish and completely cover it with fennel leaves. Pour the brandy over it and light it immediately. Serve the fish while the leaves are actually flaming.

COLD MULLET IN FENNEL VINEGAR

Red mullets	Small onion
Sprig of fennel	Bay leaf
Sprig of tarragon	Salt
Sprig of rosemary	Garlic
Flour	$\frac{1}{4}$ pt. vinegar
Olive oil	

Cover the fishes with flour and fry them in the oil, and arrange them on a dish when cooked. Next fry the chopped onion and garlic and when they are brown, sprinkle over them a tablespoonful of flour. Stir in the vinegar and chopped herbs, and cook the sauce until it is thick, then pour it over the fish. Serve this dish cold.

FENNEL WINE

1 large handful of fresh herb, or 1 small pkt dried seeds	$\frac{1}{2}$ pt. cold tea
	$2\frac{1}{2}$ lb. sugar
	1 gal. water
	$\frac{1}{2}$ oz. yeast nutrient
3 lb. beetroot	$\frac{3}{4}$ oz. yeast
3 lemons	

Boil the cleaned and sliced beetroot in the water until it is tender, and strain the liquid on to the sugar. Pour a little boiling water over the fennel and let it infuse for an hour or two. Strain this into the other liquid, add the lemon juice, cold tea and yeast, pour into fermentation jars, ferment to a finish, rack mature and bottle.

FENNEL LIQUEUR (Fenouilette)

1 lb. fennel stalks	1 tspn. nutmeg
1 lb. sugar	1 tspn. cinnamon
6 pts. brandy	1 clove

Put all the ingredients into a gallon jar and crush the fennel stalks to extract as much juice as possible. Seal it tightly and leave it in a sunny place for 1 month. Strain through a fine cloth, bottle and seal.

SACK

3 or 4 fennel roots	2 gals. water
4 lb. honey	Yeast nutrient
3 or 4 sprays rue	1 oz. yeast

Wash the roots and leaves and simmer them in some of the water for an hour. Strain the liquid on to the honey, put it back into the saucepan and simmer it for 2 hours longer, skimming when necessary. Remove it from the heat and when the liquid is lukewarm add the nutrient and yeast and pour it into fermentation jars. Stand it in a warm place. Ferment to a finish, rack, mature and bottle.

See also: Vespetro (page 208); Herbed Eggs en Cocotte (page 205).

GARLIC Fam. Lilaceae

Allium oleraceum   *Allium vineale*
   Field Garlic   Crow Garlic

These types of wild garlic have stiff grassy stems about 1 ft.
high. Crow garlic has little heads of greenish flowers, going
brown later. The flowers of field garlic are pinkish brown.
Both types of flowers carry little bulbils which fall off the
heads and from which new plants grow. Both species have
long narrow leaves, those of field garlic being roundish, of
crow garlic, cylindrical. The flavour of the root is not so
strong as that of cultivated garlic (*Allium sativum*) but it can
be used as a substitute. As garlic is, to my mind, the most
important cookery herb of all, I have included it in this book,
with several recipes, although I would normally use the
cultivated variety. Look for wild garlic growing in rough
grass, often in dunes and on sandy commons. It likes dry,
warm soil.

   The leaves of the wild variety, when young, can be chopped
and used as chives, although the flavour is definitely garlic,
not onion.

GARLIC SOUP

12 cloves garlic	Sprig sage
2 pts. water	Salt and pepper
1 tbsp. olive oil	White bread
Sprig thyme	Grated cheese

Put all the ingredients except the bread and cheese in a pan and boil them for 20 minutes. Strain the liquid through a fine strainer, and pour it into a tureen containing about a dozen small slices of bread sprinkled with grated cheese (which should be warmed just enough to make the cheese melt.) Add the olive oil, and cook it in a moderate oven until the bread has swelled and the cheese is bubbling.

GARLIC SAUCE 1

Garlic	Hazel nuts or
Olive oil	almonds

For each $\frac{1}{4}$ pint of olive oil, peel and pound about 30 nuts. Put the garlic (up to about 10 cloves according to taste) through a garlic press and blend both garlic and nuts carefully with the oil. This makes thick, strong sauce.

GARLIC SAUCE 2

6 cloves garlic	1 tbsp. lemon juice
2 thick slices bread	Water
1 pt. olive oil	Salt

Put the garlic through a garlic press, or slice it thinly and pound it well. Put the bread through a mincer, and mix it with the garlic. Add the olive oil and lemon juice very slowly, drop by drop, then add 2 tbsp. of cold water.

This strong sauce can be served with salad, aubergine fritters, or fish dishes.

GARLIC TOAST

Garlic purée (see below)	Toasted wholemeal bread
Olive oil	Breadcrumbs

Spread the garlic purée on the toast, sprinkle with breadcrumbs and olive oil. Brown it for a few minutes in a hot oven. *Garlic purée:* Blanch cloves of garlic and cook them in butter in a covered pan. Add a few spoonfuls of thick Béchamel sauce then put this all through a fine sieve or a blender before using.

GARLIC OIL

15 cloves garlic	1½ cups olive oil

Blanch the cloves of garlic, drain them and pound them in a mortar, or put them through a garlic press. Add the olive oil, and strain it through a fine cloth. Use this oil for seasoning salads.

GARLIC LOAF

2 cloves garlic	2½ oz. butter
1 French loaf	

Put the garlic through a garlic press, or chop it finely and squash it with a knife, then cream it into the butter. Cut the French loaf into ½ in. slices, or long ways, but not all the way through. Put some of the butter on each slice, press it together again, cover it with foil, and bake it in a hot oven for 15 minutes.

GARLIC BREAD

Garlic	Vinegar
Crusts of bread	Salt and pepper
Olive oil	Green salad

Rub the bread crusts with the garlic, season with oil, vinegar, salt and pepper, and add them to a fresh green salad.

GARLIC BUTTER

4 cloves garlic	½ lb. butter

First put the garlic through a press, then mix it very thoroughly with the butter, and put both through a fine sieve. Use it in sauces, forcemeats, or cold hors d'oeuvre. Finely chopped basil can be added.

GARLIC FORCEMEAT

A few cloves garlic	Yolk of 2 hard-
Butter	boiled eggs

Put the blanched cloves through a press, or chop and pound them until they are very fine (use the same amount of garlic as the 2 yolks of the eggs.) Mix the garlic and yolks carefully, and add to this, half the volume of butter. Sieve it all before use. This is very strong.

See also: Chestnuts (Freshwater Fish stuffed with); Juniper Berries (Pork Terrine with); Mushroom (Raw Mushroom Salad); Walnut and Garlic Sauce); Herb Butter (page 203); Herbed Eggs en Cocotte (page 205).

GARLIC MUSTARD Fam. Cruciferae

Alliaria petiolata
Sauce Alone, Jack by the Hedge

Garlic mustard, so called because the leaves smell strongly of garlic when crushed, was once a very common salad and flavouring herb. It grows everywhere, in semi-shade on banks and in woodlands. It has fresh-coloured green leaves, hairy underneath like nettle leaves. These are heartshaped, stalked, and toothed. The flowers are white.

Garlic mustard can be eaten chopped into bread and butter sandwiches, or boiled like spinach as a vegetable. It is also quite good in salad with meat.

GOLDEN ROD Fam. Compositae
Don't confuse this with the garden plant of the same English

Solidago virgaurea

name. Wild golden rod is a small plant, never more than 2 ft. tall, usually shorter. It is branched and downy with stalked, oblong, sometimes toothed leaves at the base of the stems, and unstalked higher up. The little, bright yellow, daisy-like flowers are in branched spikes. It is common in dry woods, and heaths and dry hedgebanks.

GOLDEN ROD WINE

1 pt. flowers	6 oranges
1 gal. water	$\frac{1}{4}$ lb. chopped raisins
3 lb. sugar	$\frac{3}{4}$ oz. yeast

Make a syrup with the water and sugar and pour it over the flowers. Add the orange juice. When it is lukewarm add the yeast and leave it for 5 days, covered, in a warm place, stirring daily. Then put the chopped raisins into a fermentation jar and strain the liquid in. Ferment to a finish, rack, mature and bottle. This will produce a sweet golden wine.

GOOSEBERRIES Fam. Grossulariaceae

Another plant familiar in cultivation, but quite common wild. It is of the same family as the currants, but has bigger green or yellowish veined fruit, on very thorny bushes.

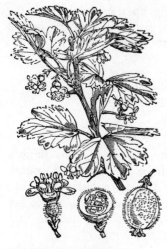

Ribes grossularia

GOOSEBERRY KETCHUP

2 qts. gooseberries	1 tbsp. ground cinnamon
2 cups vinegar	1 tbsp. cloves
3 lb. brown sugar	1 tbsp. allspice

Top and tail the gooseberries and cook them with the vinegar, sugar and spices for 2 hours, simmering slowly. Pour them into bottles and seal when cold.

GOOSEBERRY CHEESE CURD

3 lb. green gooseberries	¼ lb. butter
1½ lb. castor sugar	4 eggs
¾ pt. water	

Prepare the fruit (it is not necessary to top and tail) and cook them in the water until soft. Sieve them carefully, and put the purée into a double saucepan with the sugar, butter and lightly beaten eggs. Cook, stirring until the mixture thickens. Put it into jars and seal them as usual, but it will not keep for more than a few weeks.

GOOSEBERRY RICE

2 cupfuls gooseberries	2 pts. milk
6 oz. rice	2 oz. sugar

Wash the rice and cook it in the milk until it is soft and thick. Add the sugar well stirred in, and let it cool. Grease a basin and cover the inside of it with a layer of rice about an inch thick. Let it set well before filling up the middle with the stewed gooseberries and sugar. Put the bowl into the fridge, and when it is very cold you can turn it out to serve it.

GOOSEBERRY FRITTERS

1 pt. ripe gooseberries	2 tbsp. cream
2 oz. plain flour	2 tbsp. water
1 egg white and 2 egg	Salt
yolks	Fat for frying

Put the flour, salt, egg yolks, cream and water gradually into a bowl, stirring to make a smooth batter. Leave it to stand, then stir in the whisked egg white and the gooseberries. Take a spoonful of the mixture at a time and drop it into the hot fat. Fry the fritters until they are a golden brown, and sprinkle them with white sugar before serving.

GOOSEBERRY FOOL

1 lb. gooseberries	Tin condensed milk
Little water	

Top and tail and wash the gooseberries. Cook them in a very little water until they are soft, then put them through a sieve. When they are cold add a tin of condensed milk and blend them thoroughly. This recipe is particularly good for small wild gooseberries, as the fruit is inclined to be rather sour and the milk is very sweet.

GOOSEBERRY JAM

Gooseberries	Water
Sugar	

Top and tail the gooseberries and put them and an equal weight of sugar in a preserving pan with just enough water to stop them burning. Bring it all slowly to the boil, stirring occasionally until it reaches setting point when tested, about 40 minutes. Put the jam in warm jars and seal the usual way.

GOOSEBERRY WINE

5 lb. gooseberries	$\frac{1}{4}$ pt. cold tea
2$\frac{1}{2}$ lb. sugar	1 tspn. pectic enzyme
1 gal. water	$\frac{3}{4}$ oz. yeast
1 lemon	

Put the fruit in a container and pour boiling water over it. Crush it and mash it thoroughly for 2 days. Then strain the juice and add the lemon juice, cold tea and pectic enzyme. Make a syrup with the sugar and enough water to make up the gallon, and add it to the juice. When it is cool enough add the yeast and put it into the fermentation jar. Continue as usual. Use champagne yeast to produce a champagne type wine from this fruit.

See also: Caraway (Wine); Cherry (Wild-Jam); Mint (and Gooseberry Jelly); Sweet Cecily (Gooseberry Tart with Sweet Cecily and Balm).

GORSE Fam. Papilioniaceae

Ulex europaeus

Gorse is so common that it needs no description. It flowers all summer round but is at its best in May, when the blossom should be picked for wine. Wear tough gloves, for it is a brutal job.

GORSE WINE

$\frac{1}{2}$ gal. flowers   1 lemon
1 gal. water   2 oz. root ginger
2$\frac{1}{2}$ lb. Demerara sugar $\frac{1}{2}$ tspn. yeast nutrient
1 orange $\frac{3}{4}$ oz. yeast

Put the flowers, thinly peeled rind of the fruit and the bruised root ginger into a container and pour enough of the boiling water over them to cover. Stir well, leave for 2 days to steep,

E

and then strain and squeeze into a fermentation jar. Make syrup with enough water to fill the jar, and add it. When cool, add the yeast and yeast nutrient. Ferment to a finish, rack, mature and bottle.

GROUND ELDER Fam. Umbelliferae

Aegopodium podagraria
Goutweed, Dog Elder, Goat's Foot, Ashweed, Bishop's Weed, Bishop's Elder, Herb Gerard

This is a persistent and horrible garden weed, but it is nice to know that there is at least *one* use for it. The leaves are trifoliate with irregularly toothed, broad but pointed leaves, bright green. It grows low to the ground, but if allowed to flourish, thickens and spreads upwards and produces hollow grooved stems on which are dense white umbels of flowers.

BUTTERED GROUND ELDER

Ground elder leaves	Butter
Water	Salt and pepper

Wash the leaves in cold water and put them wet into a pan with a little butter and just enough water to stop them burning. Add a little salt and pepper. Cook gently and keep stirring. When tender, strain, and serve hot with an extra knob of butter.

HAWTHORN Fam. Rosaceae

May blossom, and the red haw berries which follow it in the autumn, are surely too well known to need description. Grow-

Crataegus monogyna
May, Whitethorn, Quickthorn

ing profusely everywhere in hedgerows, it has a characteristic smell which, for me, epitomises early summer.

Pleasant wines can be made from both blossom and berry, and when I was a child we used to pick the tiny green leaf shoots from twigs and eat them raw, and called them 'bread and cheese'. I do remember that too many had a very laxative effect!

HAW SAUCE

1½ lb. haws	½ tspn. salt
4 oz. sugar	1 oz. salt
¾ pt. vinegar	

Wash the haws well and cook them in an enamel pan with the vinegar, and simmer for 30 minutes. Put them through a sieve, or a blender and return the liquid to the pan with the sugar, salt and pepper. Boil again for 10 minutes. Pour the purée into jars and seal them firmly.

HAW JELLY

3 lb. haws	3 lemons
3 pt. water	Sugar

Wash the haws and put them in a pan with the water. Simmer them for 1 hour, pour them into a jelly bag and leave to strain overnight. Measure the juice and add 1 lb. of sugar and the juice of 1 lemon to each pint. Boil until the jelly sets, and put into jars and seal.

HAWTHORNBERRY WINE

2 lb. haws	1 lemon
2½/3 lb. sugar	1 gal. water
2 oranges	¾ oz. yeast

Put the berries in a container and mash them, then pour on enough of the boiling water to cover them. Leave them for 4 days, mashing and stirring daily. Strain off on to the thinly peeled rinds of the fruit, and the juice, and put into a fermentation jar. Prepare syrup with the sugar and enough water to make up the gallon. Add it to the juices, and when cool, add the yeast. Continue as usual.

HAWTHORN BLOSSOM OR MAYFLOWER WINE

1 gal. hawthorn blossom	1 lemon
2 lb. sugar	¾ oz. yeast
1 gal. water	½ tspn. yeast nutrient

Put the blossom in a container with the thinly peeled rind of the lemon and its juice. Pour over enough boiling water to cover. After 3 days, strain the liquid into a fermentation jar and make a syrup with the sugar and the rest of the gallon of water. Add the syrup, and when cool, add yeast nutrient and yeast. Ferment to a finish, rack, mature and bottle.

This simple recipe without raisins or other additions, makes a very lightly flavoured blossom wine; sweet or dry according to the amount of sugar used. 3 lb. will make a medium wine.

HAWTHORN BRANDY

May blossoms	Sugar
Brandy	

Fill a kilner jar with mayflowers and top it up with brandy, shaking it well and making sure no air remains in the jar. Let it stand for 3 weeks, strain off the liqueur and sweeten it to taste with white sugar.

See also: Green Dumplings (page 206).

HAZEL NUTS Fam. Corylaceae

A small deciduous tree, which grows either in hedgerows or in woods, where it is usually coppiced or cut back and allowed

Corylus avellana
Cob nuts

to regrow; the straight sticks having many uses. It has brownish-red smooth bark, and produces small, pale yellow tails or male catkins in very early spring. The leaves are pointed and oval, downy when they appear in spring. The nuts grow from the female catkins and are encased in thick green husks. Common everywhere, particularly in S.E. England.

Hazel nuts are only occasionally blanched. To grind them, put them in a coffee or cheese grinder.

HAZEL NUT BUTTER
2½ oz. blanched hazelnuts   Little water
10 tbsp. butter

Pound the blanched nuts into a fine paste, add a few drops of water to stop them turning into oil. Add the butter, and rub the mixture through a fine sieve. This can be used as a garnish for hors d'oeuvre, in soups and some white sauces.

HAZEL NUT CAKE 1
4 oz. ground hazel nuts   ¼ tspn. baking powder
3 eggs   Flavoured butter
3½ oz. sugar   icing
2 tbsp. breadcrumbs

Beat the egg yolks and sugar together thoroughly, add the nuts, breadcrumbs and baking powder, and fold in the whipped egg whites. Put the mixture into a buttered tin and bake it for ¾ hour in a slow oven. When the cake is cool, it can be iced with any flavoured icing that you think would go well with it. Coffee is especially good.

HAZEL NUT CAKE 2

10 oz. finely ground hazel nuts	1 tbsp. dried potato flour or flakes
10 oz. brown sugar	Egg white
6 oz. ground almonds	Vanilla essence

Mix the hazelnuts, almonds, sugar and potato flour to a paste and bind them with the egg white and add a few drops of vanilla essence. Spread this mixture on a well-greased baking tin about ¼ in. thick and cook it in a moderate oven. When cold, it can be decorated with icing and more whole nuts.

HONEYED HAZEL NUTS

8 oz. chopped hazel nuts	1 cup honey
7 oz. S.R. flour	5 oz. sugar
2 eggs	2 tspn. ground ginger
	Salt

Beat the eggs, then work in the flour and a pinch of salt. Roll this out into long pieces about ½ inch thick, and cut it into cubes. Put the honey, sugar and ginger into a saucepan and bring them to the boil. Drop in the pieces of dough. Don't put too many in at a time. Reduce the heat and cook them gently for about ½ hour without stirring. Lift them on to a flat tin with a shallow rim upon which the nuts have been sprinkled, and pour the syrup over the top. When it is all cool and set, cut it into squares.

CANDIED HAZEL NUTS

Hazel nuts	Sugar
Thin sugar syrup	Icing sugar

Blanch the nuts and skin them. Simmer the nuts in the syrup for an hour. Let them cool, then add more sugar, simmer for another hour, and again allow them to cool. Repeat this process adding sugar each time until the syrup is so thick that when it cools it becomes candy. Take out the nuts before the syrup cools to this consistency; put them on a tray and dust them well with powdered sugar, then dry them in the hot sun or in a very slow oven. The syrup can be used up for any other preserve.

See also : Garlic (Sauce 1).

HONEYSUCKLE Fam. Caprifoliaceae

Lonicera peryclymenum

Very well known, and common, honeysuckle climbs on other trees and bushes, and has sweet-scented cream, buff and crimson flowers with long slender tubes. These flowers make a pleasant wine.

HONEYSUCKLE WINE

2 pts blossom	1 gal. water
2½ lb. sugar	½ tspn. nutrient
1 lemon	1 Campden tablet
1 orange	½ oz. yeast

Use fully opened flowers and put them in a container with a Campden tablet. Pour over enough boiling water to cover, and stir well. Leave the must covered for 2 days, stirring several times. Make a syrup with the rest of the water, and strain the liquid from the blossoms into this. When cool, add the rind of the fruit peeled thin without white pith, and the juice of the fruit, the nutrient and the yeast. Put it all into a fermentation jar, ferment to a finish, rack, mature and bottle.

HOPS Fam. Cannabinaceae

Humulus lupulus

Hops, widely cultivated for beer making, are fairly common wild, especially in hop growing districts in S.E. England. Hops are perennial, but die right back in the winter to appear again each summer, climbing clockwise round other bushes, usually in hedgerows. They have coarsely toothed leaves, rather like ivy, only pale green. The female flowers grow into the cone shaped green heads which are the part used to flavour beer. The male flowers are branched catkins, and these small edible flower shoots and tips should be picked from the woody stems.

The petals of the female flowers, dried, are used to make hop wine and to flavour home-made beer and mead.

BUTTERED HOP

Small male flower	Butter
shoots and tips	Cream, or veal
Salted water	stock
Lemon juice	

Boil the shoots in salted water with a few drops of lemon juice. Then toss them in butter; or toss them in butter and simmer them in cream; or toss them in butter and simmer them for a few moments in concentrated veal stock.

When cooked like this they can be used as a garnish for omelettes. In Belgium they are served as a vegetable garnished with poached eggs, and croutons of bread cut in elaborate shapes and fried in butter.

HOP WINE

3 oz. dried hops or 9
   handfuls fresh hops
3 lb. sugar
1 gal. water
1 oz. ginger

1 lemon, 1 orange
$\frac{1}{4}$ lb. raisins
$\frac{1}{2}$ tspn. yeast nutrient
$\frac{3}{4}$ oz. yeast

Bruise the ginger and boil it with the hops in the water for 1 hour. Strain the liquid and pour it over $2\frac{1}{2}$ lb. sugar and the orange and lemon juice. Put this into a fermentation jar and when cool add the yeast. When fermentation ceases, rack the liquid into another container, add the last $\frac{1}{2}$ lb. sugar and the raisins. Bung the container tightly and after another 6 months, rack again and bottle.

This is a little tricky as these additions may restart fermentation which will blow the bung. They should produce just sufficient fermentation to make a sparkling and unusually flavoured wine.

MEAD

5 lb. honey including wax
2 oz. dried hops
3 gal. water

Juice of 2 lemons
1 tspn. yeast nutrient
2 oz. yeast

Dissolve the honey in the water and add the hops and simmer for 1 hour. Strain into fermentation jars, add the lemon juice and when cool add the yeast and nutrient.

The proportions of honey and hops can be varied to taste. Keep the mead as long as possible before drinking, for it improves with keeping.

HOP ALE (Old recipe)

4 oz. dried hops
2 oz. gentian root
3 lb. dark brown sugar

2 oz. dandelion root
6 gal. water
3 tbsp. yeast

Boil the herbs in the water for 2½ hours. Strain the lukewarm liquid on to the sugar and add the yeast. Stir well and cover. Next day rack carefully, into a cask, leaving the sediment behind. Bung it tightly, and after a few days the brew is ready to drink.

LIGHT ALE

2 oz. dried hops
1½ lb. white sugar
2 lb. malt extract

2 gal. water
1 oz. yeast

Put the malt and sugar into a polythene bucket. Boil the hops in a pan of water for ½ hour and strain the liquid into the bucket. Repeat this process until the bucket is full to within 2 in. of the top. When the 'wort' is cool, add the yeast. Leave, lightly covered for a week when the fermentation should be forming a ring on the surface of the wort, and rack into another bucket. Leave it for a couple of days longer to allow the sediment to settle again. Then siphon the beer into screw-top beer bottles, in which you have put ¼ tspn. of sugar (per pint). Screw the tops down. After a fortnight the beer should be ready to drink, and will be clear and sparkling with a good head on it.

See also: Metheglin (page 207).

HORSERADISH Fam. Cruciferae

Armoracia rusticana

Horseradish grows anywhere on rich, dry soil, in the sunshine, in great clumps, and the dark green leaves look like big dock leaves. The roots, (particularly the outsides of them) are the part used. You will have to dig well down with a spade or fork to get them out, pulling will only result in breaking off the plant at ground level.

During the summer, however, you can also eat young horseradish leaves chopped or minced and mixed with green salads.

The strong hot flavour of horseradish roots is well known, but apart from accompanying beef dishes of all kinds, it is also good with shellfish dishes, smoked trout and avocado pears. It can also be grated and mixed with finely chopped hard-boiled eggs, seasoned with lemon juice, herbs and salt.

HORSERADISH AND AVOCADO PEARS

Grated horseradish	Tarragon
Melted butter or	Parsley
whipped cream	Chervil
Salt	Avocado pears

Mix all the ingredients and put them into halved avocado pears.

HORSERADISH SAUCE 1

Grated horseradish	Vinegar
Breadcrumbs	Thick cream
Little milk	Salt
Sugar	

Mix the horseradish with breadcrumbs which have been soaked in milk and squeezed as dry as possible. Season with salt and sugar and add thick cream and a little vinegar.

HORSERADISH SAUCE 2

1 pt. white sauce	Little lemon juice
$\frac{1}{4}$ horseradish root	Salt
Little milk	

Peel and grate the horseradish, mix it with a little milk and add it to the hot white sauce. Do not let it boil. Season to taste with salt and lemon juice.

HORSERADISH SAUCE 3

1 oz. grated horseradish	1 tspn. castor sugar
Wineglass of wine vinegar	1 tbsp. cream
	Salt and pepper

Mix all the ingredients very thoroughly in a bowl. Oil can be used instead of cream, and in this case add some finely grated orange peel.

HORSERADISH CANAPES

Pumpernickel	Hard boiled eggs
English mustard	Butter
Grated horseradish	Chopped chives

Blend together the butter, mustard and chives and spread them on the pumpernickel. Cover with grated horseradish and add a border of chopped hard boiled eggs.

HORSERADISH DIP

3 oz. Philadelphia cream cheese	1 tbsp. sherry
2 to 3 tspn. grated horseradish	1 dspn. salad cream
	Salt and pepper
	Cayenne pepper

Mix all the ingredients, except the cayenne, very thoroughly. If the dip is not runny enough add a little cream or top of the milk. Make it hotter or milder by adjusting the amount of horseradish. Sprinkle the dip with cayenne just before serving.

COLE SLAW

Raw cabbage	Horseradish
Grated apple	Salad cream
Sultanas	Salt and pepper
Grated celery	

Make up the cole slaw with the vegetables in whatever proportion you like, and add enough salad cream to coat all the pieces. Sprinkle on a teaspoonful of horseradish on with the seasoning and mix it well into the salad.

HORSERADISH AND HAM

1 tbsp. grated horseradish	Lemon juice
4 slices ham	Sugar
1 tbsp. cream	Salt

Mix the horseradish with the cream, add a little salt, sugar and lemon juice. Fold the ham into shapes, and spread the horseradish mixture over them.

HORSERADISH AND MACKEREL

4 mackerel	Wineglassful vinegar
3 tbsp. horseradish sauce	$\frac{1}{4}$ tspn. mixed herbs
1 small chopped onion	1 bay leaf
2 cooking apples	Salt and pepper
$\frac{1}{2}$ pt. water	

Clean, scale and fillet the mackerel and simmer the bones with the vinegar, water, onion, herbs and salt and pepper for about 20 minutes. Strain the liquor into a saucepan and put the rolled up fillets of fish in the liquid. Secure them in rolls with tooth picks. Simmer them gently for 15 minutes and serve them with grated apple and horseradish sprinkled on top.
See also: Hot Sauce (page 205).

JUNIPER Fam. Cupressaceae

> '... So thik the bewis and the leves grene
> Beschadit all the aleyes that there were,
> And middis everye herbere might be sene
> That scharpe grene swete jenepere,
> Growing so faire with branchis here and there,
> That, as it semit to a lif without,
> The bewis spred the herbere all about.'
>   King James I of Scotland, *The Kingis Quhair.*

Juniper bushes are about waist high, and very prickly. Common on chalk downs, heaths and sometimes in woods. The leaves are in whorls of three, and the berries, which take 3 years to ripen, can be found at all stages of ripeness on each female bush. They are best identified by their unmistakable smell of gin. Juniper growing in this country does not have

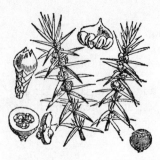

Juniperus communis

such a strong smell and flavour as that growing in more southern climates.

Only pick the berries when they are black in the autumn. Use them fresh or dried, and keep them in a glass jar for future use.

Juniper is said to counteract the smell of garlic on your breath, but really only replaces it with the smell of gin!

Juniper goes well with other herbs, parsley, thyme, garlic, etc., so can be added to stuffings, and with wine and brandy in meat dishes.

Apart from smelling of gin, juniper berries also taste of it, in fact they are one of its main flavouring ingredients. They go well with sauerkraut, meat pickled in brine, and with any rich food such as hare, venison and pork. Wild duck or grouse are sometimes part boiled before being roasted, and juniper berries, lemon, bay leaf and good beef stock may be added to the boiling liquid. This is strained and used to make the gravy.

Laplanders make a herb tea of juniper berries. Use 12 to 18 crushed berries per cup, bring to the boil and simmer for 15 minutes.

PORK TERRINE WITH JUNIPER BERRIES

3 chump chops or	1 apple
leg fillets	10 juniper berries
2 large onions	1 clove garlic
2 large potatoes	Ham or streaky
1 wineglass white	bacon
wine or cider	Salt and pepper

Slice the onions, apples and potatoes thinly. Put half the onion in the bottom of a casserole, then a layer of half the potato and half the apple. Sprinkle 5 juniper berries on this. Put a piece of garlic on each chop, and lay them in the casserole. Add another layer of potatoes, the rest of the apple, juniper berries and onion. Cover the lot with rashers of bacon or slices of ham, and pour in the wine. Put on a lid of baking foil and then the casserole lid, so that all is well sealed, and cook in a low oven for 3 hours. The meat should be butter tender and the vegetables very soft. Most of the wine will have been used, but there should be a little gravy left. Check after about 2½ hours, and add a little more wine if necessary.

LATWERGE

Juniper berries   Sugar
Water

This is a German juniper conserve, eaten with cold meat. Cook the berries in a little water until they are soft but not broken. Then press the pulp through a sieve and add 3 times its weight of sugar. Beat it all well together and reheat the mixture, stirring constantly until it reaches setting point.

JUNIPER LIQUEUR

1 qt. juniper   2 lb. sugar
  berries   Little water
1 qt. brandy

Dissolve the sugar in a little water to make a syrup, pour this over the berries and add the alcohol. Put it into a sealed jar and shake it from time to time for a week or longer. Strain the liqueur carefully and bottle the liquid. The longer this liqueur is left the better, so hide it away for a year or two! See also: Highland Bitters (page 208).

LAVER Fam. Chlorophyceae/Fam. Rhodophyceae

Both green and red laver are gathered for food, although the latter is by far the better. Both grow in rock pools, the green laver near the low tide line. Green laver is translucent, bright green with short wide fronds up to 6 in. long; red laver also has thin, wide-lobed fronds, up to 10 in. long.

    Laver begins to grow in the early spring and is at its best in April and May. The fronds should be laid out to dry under

Porphyra umbilicalis
Red Laver

Ulva lactuca
Green Laver

cover, but where the fresh air can flow over them. The best laver is cured on a floor of sand that has taken 7 years to grow the right bacterial flora for perfect curing. It is turned daily.

LAVER BREAD

Dried laver
Cold water

Salt or bicarbonate
of soda

Wash the dried seaweed carefully, then steep it for a few hours in cold water, with a little salt or bicarbonate of soda, to get rid of some of the bitterness. Cover it with fresh water in a thick aluminium pan and boil it gently to a jelly. When it is completely cooked, it goes dark green. Put it in earthenware jars when it is quite cool, where it will keep for 2 to 3 weeks. Eat this jelly on bread or oatcakes.

LAVER SAUCE 1

Laver bread
Pepper

Lemon juice

Prepare the laver bread as in the above recipe, and add pepper and lemon juice to it. Serve the sauce very hot with roast mutton.

LAVER SAUCE 2

$\frac{1}{2}$ pt. laver bread
Juice of 2 lemons
1 tbsp. redcurrant
jelly

4 tbsp. beef stock
Little castor
sugar

Put all the ingredients except the laver bread in a pan and boil them for about 10 minutes. Keep skimming, then mix in the prepared laver, boil everything up again, put it all through a sieve or blender, and eat it as a sauce with roast lamb or venison.

LAVER SAUCE 3

1 lb. laver bread	Thick mutton gravy
2 oz. butter	Lemon juice

Mix all the ingredients together, and serve the sauce steaming hot with the hot meat.

BREAKFAST LAVER CAKES

Laver bread	Oatmeal (finely
Bacon fat	ground)

This is the traditional Welsh way of eating laver. Mix the laver with some oatmeal, make it into little flat cakes, and fry them for breakfast, preferably with sausages.

SAVOURY LAVER

Laver bread	Olive oil
Vinegar or lemon juice	Salt and pepper

Mix the laver bread with vinegar or lemon juice, a few drops of olive oil, pepper and salt and serve it cold on toast.

SLOKAN

Laver bread	Potatoes
Butter	Salted water
Salt and pepper	

Prepare the laver bread in the usual way, then put it in a pan with a little salted water. Heat it, beating it well, heat and beat it again. Do this until the seaweed is a complete pulp. Do not let it boil. Add salt, pepper and a knob of butter. Serve it hot with mashed potatoes.

SEAWEED SOUP

Laver bread	Butter
Milk	Vinegar or lemon
Pepper	juice

Stew the prepared laver in enough milk to make a soup of the right consistency, rubbing it hard with a wooden spoon until it is quit tender. It can be strained or the pieces of laver left in the soup. Season it with pepper, add some butter, and vinegar or lemon juice to taste.

Lime Fam. Tiliaceae

Tilia europaea

There are several species of lime tree, characterised by the very sweet scented, yellowish flowers which hang down in clusters. The leaves are wide but thin, delicate green, and slightly hairy underneath.

LIME TEA

Gather the lime flowers for making tea in June and July. They should be carefully dried before use. 1 tspn. of lime flowers and 1 for the pot. Never boil the tea, or the liquid will turn red, and do not steep it for longer than 3 or 4 minutes. It can be drunk either hot or cold, and sweetened if necessary with honey.

LIME BLOSSOM WINE

2 pts. lime flowers	1 lemon
3 lb. sugar	½ tspn. nutrient
1 gal. water	¾ oz. yeast

Put the flowers into a saucepan with the thinly-peeled lemon rind and simmer for 10 minutes. Strain the liquid on to the sugar and the lemon juice. When cool put into a fermentation jar with the nutrient and yeast. Continue as usual.

LOVAGE Fam. Umbelliferae

Ligusticum scoticum

The only lovage which grows wild in this country can be found on rocky cliffs in Scotland and in Northumberland and Northern Ireland and is a short version of true lovage, being only 18 in. high. It has stiff, ribbed, purple stems, and rather leathery, shiny bright-green, trifoliate leaves. The umbels of flowers are white. When crushed the plant smells strongly of celery. The smell is a little musky. Cultivated lovage grows up to 7 ft. high and can occasionally be found as an escape, for it grows easily enough in this country.

Lovage stems can be candied like angelica or used fresh as a celery-type vegetable. The leaves and seeds can be used fresh for flavouring (but use them sparingly as they have a stronger flavour than celery), and the seeds are dried. These seeds have similar uses to fennel or dill, on bread, biscuits and meat. The Greeks and Romans chewed them just because they liked them!

Pick lovage leaves before the plant flowers, and use them either fresh or dried. They and the seeds are good in hors-d'oeuvre, salads, soups, stews, sauces, meat and fish dishes, poultry and game dishes, with other vegetables or on cakes and biscuits. The seeds go well in mixed fruit salads and game stews, but should be removed before the dish is served.

LOVAGE SOUP

1 lb. potatoes
1 onion
2 tbsp. dried or fresh
   lovage
2 pts. stock
½ oz. butter

1 tspn. chopped
   parsley
½ pt. milk
½ oz. flour
Salt

Peel and slice the onion and potatoes, then sauté the onions gently in the butter, add the lovage, potatoes, sprinkle in the flour and cook for a little longer. Add the stock and salt gradually, stirring all the time, and simmer for 20 minutes, until the potatoes are completely broken down. Add the milk, and put it all through a sieve or blender. Heat the mixture up again before serving it sprinkled with chopped parsley.

MARJORAM Fam. Labiatae

Origanum vulgare

Marjoram grows on chalk downs and limestone, up to about 2 ft. high, on slender stems, which branch high up and have oval, slightly toothed leaves of fairly dark green. The heads of many buds turn to purple two-lipped flowers.

There are several species of cultivated marjorum and oregano and it is a very popular herb in the Mediterranean. The wild variety is not quite so pungent and can be used fresh or dried for any of the uses of the cultivated type. It has a sweet spicy flavour. The leaves are used for flavouring all meat dishes, poultry, vegetables, salads, fish, cheese and egg dishes, and in milk puddings and milk shakes. The Italians use it to flavour tomato, cheese, beans, zucchini (courgettes), fish, meat shellfish, aubergines, and it is also used with chilli powder to flavour chilli beans or chilli con carne. Oregano is a herb which goes well with so many things.

The flavour is quite strong, so experiment carefully to find the quantities to use. It is excellent in stuffings for meat or poultry.

BEEF IN MARJORAM SAUCE

1–2 lb. stewing beef	1 chopped onion
	Stock
1 tspn. fresh or dried marjoram	1 tbsp. flour
	Butter
$\frac{1}{4}$ pt. sour cream or yoghurt	Salt and pepper

Sauté the onion in the butter until golden. Roll the pieces of meat in seasoned flour and brown them with the onions. Season this to taste, transfer it to a casserole, pour the stock over it and cook it in a medium oven until the meat is tender. Add the marjoram $\frac{1}{2}$ hour before serving the stew, and stir in the sour cream at the last minute.

See also: Mushroom Croquettes (page 161); Herb Wine (page 206); Herbed Eggs en Cocotte (page 205); Metheglin (page 207).

MEADOWSWEET Fam. Rosaceae

Filipendula ulmaria

A very common plant which grows in damp meadows, along hedgerows and near streams. The rich creamy-white flowers smell rather like may blossom. The leaves which grow opposite each other are green above and silvery green below. The plant is up to 2 ft. tall.

Meadowsweet does not have many culinary uses except as a flavouring, added to country wines and beers, and in jams, jellies and stewed fruit. Use one or two flowers with these sweet dishes.

Meadowsweet blossom tea can be made from the dried flowers, and the plant also makes a good, well-flavoured light wine.

MEADOWSWEET WINE

1 gal. flowers $\frac{1}{4}$ pt. cold tea
$\frac{1}{2}$ lb. raisins 1 gal. water
1 lemon $\frac{3}{4}$ oz. yeast
$2\frac{1}{2}$ lb. sugar

Put the flower heads in a container and pour boiling water over them. Stir thoroughly and leave for 3 days, stirring frequently. Strain the liquid on to the sugar and stir until the sugar has dissolved. Add the juice of the lemon, the cold tea, the chopped raisins and the yeast, and put the lot into a fermentation jar. Finish as usual.

MEDLAR Fam. Rosaceae

Mespilus germanica

Wild medlar is a thorny shrub, but most medlars that you may find are escapes, growing from seeds carried by birds. The pointed, downy, untoothed leaves turn yellow in autumn, and the single flowers are white with red anthers and long leaf-like sepals, which stay on the round, brown fruit. The fruit itself remains on the tree long after the leaves have fallen.

MEDLAR PUDDING

2 lb. medlars
¾ lb. sugar to each
   pint of juice
1 pt. water

Lemon juice
Vanilla essence
Whipped cream

Peel, core and cut up the ripe medlars, and add them to the water with a little lemon juice. Cook them to a pulp, then rub them through a sieve or break it down in a blender. To each pint of juice add ¾ lb. sugar. Boil this quickly, skimming all the time, and when it is the consistency of thick cream, let it cool a little, then add a few drops of vanilla essence. Pour it into a serving dish with dollops of whipped cream on top.

This mixture can be made into a mould by adding to each pint of purée ½ oz. of gelatine while it is still warm. Put it in the fridge to set before turning it out.

COMPOTE OF MEDLARS

Medlars	Syrup (1 cup water
Rind of ½ lemon	to 1 lb. sugar)

Peel the fruit and cook it in the syrup, with the lemon rind, until the medlars are whole but spongy. Lift the fruit out carefully and strain the juice over them.

MEDLAR WINE

8 lb. medlars	1 gal. water
½ lb. raisins	Pectozyme
Campden tablet	¾ oz. yeast
2½ lb. sugar	

Use only ripe, soft fruit, which should be washed and crushed, with the chopped raisins. Pour the boiling water over the fruit, add the Campden tablet and pectozyme and stir thoroughly. Leave it for 4 days, strain off the liquid on to the sugar, add the yeast and put the must into a fermentation jar. Finish as usual.

MELILOT Fam. Leguminosae

Melilotus officinalis

Melilot leaves look like clover leaves, but longer, and when the plant comes up in early summer it is rich, bright green. It grows up to 4 ft. high and is common in fields and waste places and in sand dunes or on sandy soil. Later in summer the spikes of yellow flowers appear and fill the air with honey scent, and as the plant matures it smells of new-mown hay. It is best used dried.

Melilot can be used to flavour herb beers. Rabbit, cooked, wrapped in or stuffed with melilot, gains a sweet, hay-like flavour.

MILFOIL Fam. Compositae

Achillea millefolium
Yarrow

A dark green plant growing up to 18 in. high. This is a common plant which grows everywhere in grassy places. The leaves are long and fernlike, the flower heads are in umbels, rather flat with many small white flowers with darker centres. It is a stiff little plant covered with down. The young leaves are used as a salad vegetable, or chopped to replace chervil or parsley as a garnish.
See also: Fresh Spring Herb Soup (page 204).

MINT Fam. Mentha

Mentha rotundifolia
Applemint

M. piperita
Peppermint

M. Spicata
Spearmint

M. Aquatica
Water Mint

Water mint is the commonest wild species, but mints cross-breed and grow so easily that several varieties which are better for cooking can be found wild, usually as escapes. Spearmint, everywhere, peppermint in the south and west; applemint in the south-west. Each has a slightly different flavour and you can by experimentation find the best uses for any particular mint which grows wild in your part of the country.

Water mint is purplish green and hairy and has lilac-red flowers, and oval, toothed leaves growing to a point. It has a characteristic pungent mint-and-mud smell when crushed. The other mints are the same as the cultivated varieties, identifiable by their mint smells.

Young fresh vegetables such as carrots, green peas, potatoes, spinach and runner beans are all greatly improved in flavour if melted butter and finely chopped fresh or dried mint is sprinkled over them before serving.

Mint is also excellent used in fruit juices, fruit cups, fruit and vegetable salads, soups, sauces, jellies and jams. 1½ tspn. of crushed mint added to plain Madeira cake mixture gives it an unusual flavour.

Best of all is mint sauce to eat with lamb, especially if it is made with lemon or cider or wine vinegar, which will not mask the mint flavour as does strong malt vinegar. Mint jelly made with apple or crabapple to help it set, or with gelatine, is also excellent with lamb.

MINT CHUTNEY

4 oz. fresh mint
1 fresh green chilli
1 tspn. sugar

1 onion
Juice of ¼ lemon
¼ tspn. salt

Chop or mince the mint leaves very finely. Add the other ingredients and mix them well. Eat it with curry on the day it is made.

MINT AND ORANGE SALAD

4 oranges
2 tbsp. mint
1 tbsp. sherry

1 tbsp. lemon juice
Sugar to taste

To the juice and flesh of the oranges add the sugar and finely chopped mint. Flavour with the sherry and lemon juice, and garnish with more mint leaves.

MINT PASTY

Mint	Currants
Brown sugar	Pastry

In the north of England, this is a very popular pasty. Use equal quantities of fresh chopped mint, brown sugar and currants, mix them well together and put them in pastry cases as filling. Cook in a moderate oven until the pastry is golden.

MINT AND GOOSEBERRY JELLY

Gooseberries	Mint
Sugar	Wine vinegar

Make jelly from ripe yellow gooseberries. Use ¼ pt. of water per 1 lb. of fruit. Stew the berries in the water until they are mushy, then strain off the juice without crushing the fruit. Add ¾ lb. of sugar, 4 tbsp. of finely-chopped mint and a tablespoonful of wine vinegar, per pint of juice, and boil it to setting point. (Do not use malt vinegar, as it is too strongly flavoured.) This jelly goes very well with roast lamb.

MINT AND RHUBARB JELLY

Rhubarb	Sugar
Mint	Water

Cut the rhubarb into cubes. Stew it in a little water until it is soft, then strain it through a fine sieve. To each pint of juice add 1 lb. of sugar and a big handful of fresh mint tied in a bunch. Boil again and when the jelly reaches setting point, remove the mint, pour the jelly into small jars and seal them. Serve it with lamb.

MINT TEA

8 tbsp. chopped dried mint	1 pt. water

Make this tea the same way as any other kind of tea, and leave it to stand for 5 minutes before pouring it out. Sweeten it with sugar or honey. A slice of lemon can be added. The strength of the tea depends very much on the time of the year when the mint was picked.

PEPPERMINT MILK

1 tbsp. peppermint leaves	$\frac{1}{2}$ pt. milk

Pour the boiling milk over the finely chopped mint leaves, and let it stand for 5 minutes, then strain it and serve it very hot. A good late drink if you have a cold.

AMERICAN MINT JULEP

Mint	Crushed ice
Peach brandy and ordinary brandy	Piece pineapple White sugar

Put a dozen sprigs of mint into a tumbler with a spoonful of white sugar. Fill the glass one third full with equal proportions of peach brandy and ordinary brandy, then top it right up with crushed ice. Rub round the rim of the glass with the pineapple.

MINT JULEP

Brandy	Sprigs of fresh mint
Sugar	
Ice	

Pour brandy on to sugar and broken ice and add some sprigs of fresh mint, bruised or crushed.

MINT WINE

2 pts. mint leaves	$\frac{1}{4}$ pt. cold tea
2 lemons	1 tspn. yeast nutrient
1 gal. water	$\frac{3}{4}$ oz. yeast
3 lb. sugar	

Put the mint into a container and pour boiling water over it. Mash well, cover and leave it for 2 days. Squeeze and strain all the juice out and make the sugar into a syrup. Combine the syrup, mint juice, cold tea, lemon juice, nutrient and yeast and put them into a fermentation jar. Finish as usual.

See also: Fennel (and Cucumber Salad); Nettles (Nettle

Country Pudding); and Herb Wine (page 206); Herbed Eggs en Cocotte (page 205).

MOREL Fam. Discomycetes

Morchella esculenta

There are several species of morel native to this country, and they are easy to identify. They have brittle, short white mealy hollow stalks and the hollow heads are like irregular honeycombs or sponges. The fungus stands up from the ground and can vary in colour from ochre yellow to grey and dark brown, and in shape from rounded to conical.

Wash them well before eating them. They are good as flavouring in soups and stews, and can be stuffed with a savoury mixture of minced meat and herbs and baked in a covered dish in the oven.

MUSHROOMS Fam. Agaricales

Agaricus campestris

The common field mushroom has a white cap and is slightly silky on top. When young the fungus is round, and the stout stem has the thin white membrane at the top. The gills of the cap are whitish-pink, then salmon-pink, and turn coffee coloured then chocolate coloured as the mushroom flattens out and grows to ripeness. The ripe spores are purplish-black, never a real brown. There is no need to peel mushrooms before eating them except to remove dirt which cannot be brushed or washed off. The stems should be trimmed at the base and used as flavouring.

PICKLED MUSHROOMS 1

Mushrooms	Salt
Vinegar	Cayenne pepper

Use small button mushrooms and clean them by rubbing them with a damp cloth dipped in salt. Put them in a saucepan on a *very* low heat; take care that as the moisture runs out they do not burn. When this moisture has been re-absorbed, cover them with vinegar, leave this to simmer slowly. Put them in jars and seal when cold.

PICKLED MUSHROOMS 2

1 lb. small mushrooms	1 tspn. salt
White malt vinegar	1 tspn. ginger
$\frac{1}{2}$ oz. chopped onion	2 blades mace
4 crushed peppercorns	

Wash the mushrooms, trim the stalks, and cut into slices any larger ones. Put them in a saucepan and just cover them with vinegar. Put in the other ingredients, bring to the boil and cover the pan and simmer it slowly for 15 minutes. Put the strained mushrooms in jars, and pour over them enough of the hot vinegar to cover them. Seal the jars, and store them for a couple of weeks before using.

MUSHROOM KETCHUP

Mushrooms	Mixed spice
Salt and pepper	Onion

Break up large black mushrooms and put them in an earthen-ware jar, cover them with salt and leave them in a cool place

for 3 days. Stir them frequently with a wooden spoon. Strain
the liquid into a saucepan and simmer it for 30 minutes. Add
the pepper, mixed spice and onion (optional). When it is
quite cold, strain it again, and put it into bottles.

To thicken the sauce, mix in a little plain flour separately
with some of the cool liquid, add the hot liquid to it and simmer it until it is the right consistency, stirring all the time.

MUSHROOMS IN WINE

1 lb. mushrooms	1 tspn. parsley
1 tomato	½ cup dry white wine
4 tbsp. butter	Salt and pepper

Slice the cleaned mushrooms and peel and chop the tomato.
Put these in the butter and fry them. Add the chopped parsley
and cook it for another 5 minutes, stirring all the time. Add
the wine, and salt and pepper to taste. Heat it all again for 3
minutes, and serve it very hot.

MUSHROOMS IN YOGHURT

1 lb. mushrooms	1 cup yoghurt
1 minced onion	4 tbsp. parsley
3 tbsp. butter	1 tspn. salt, pepper
⅓ cup water	and paprika

Slice the cleaned mushrooms. Fry the onion in the butter until
it is golden. Add the mushrooms and water and cook gently
for about 15 minutes. Add more water if necessary. Add salt,
pepper, paprika and half the chopped parsley, and stir in the
yoghurt. Serve the dish with the rest of the parsley as garnish.

RAW MUSHROOM SALAD

¼ lb. mushrooms	1 clove garlic
¼ pt. olive oil	Salt and black
2 tbsp. lemon juice	pepper
3 tbsp. parsley	

Wash and dry the mushrooms and slice them thinly. Pour on
to them the lemon juice, pressed or finely chopped garlic, olive
oil and pepper, and add the salt just before serving. This salad
should be made some hours before serving, as it soaks up a

lot of oil. A little more can be added at the last minute if necessary.

This is a good 'sambal' to eat with a hot curry.

MUSHROOM DUMPLINGS

2 oz. mushrooms	1 tbsp. cornflour
1 egg	1½ oz. breadcrumbs
1½ oz. butter	Salt

Clean and chop the mushrooms. Fry them in ½ oz. butter. Cream the rest of the butter, add the egg, cornflour, salt and the cooled mushrooms. Add enough breadcrumbs to make a smooth dough. Leave it to stand for ½ hour, then shape small dumplings and cook them in boiling salted water or soup.

MUSHROOM CROQUETTES

½ lb. mushrooms	2 eggs
1 small onion	Marjoram
4 slices of stale	1½ oz. breadcrumbs
bread	2 oz. fat for frying
1 oz. butter	

Clean the mushrooms and chop them. Soak the bread in water then squeeze out all the liquid. Fry the mushrooms in the fat with the finely chopped onion. Add the eggs and bread, and season it with salt and marjoram. Shape the mixture into rissoles, coat them with breadcrumbs, and fry them in the hot fat until they are brown.

MUSHROOM AND CRAB

1 crab	2 egg yolks
¼ lb. mushrooms	2 tbsp. sherry
2 oz. butter	Paprika
2 tbsp. flour	Salt
1 tspn. parsley	Breadcrumbs
1 cup stock	Melted butter

Make a sauce of the butter, flour and stock, add the egg yolks, salt and paprika to taste, and the crab meat and the mushrooms. Boil this gently for a few minutes before adding the finely chopped parsley and sherry. Put it on one side to cool. Place the mixture into cleaned crab shells, sprinkle them with bread-

F

crumbs and melted butter and bake them in a moderate oven until the breadcrumbs are brown.

MUSHROOM AND CELERY PIE

6 oz. mushrooms	1 onion
1 head wild celery	Paprika
$\frac{1}{2}$ pt. milk	Salt and pepper
1 oz. flour	2 oz. grated cheese
2 oz. butter	Breadcrumbs

Clean and slice the mushrooms and cook them gently in the milk. Strain off the milk and put the mushrooms into a casserole. Chop the onion and celery and fry them gently in the butter for a few minutes. Blend in the flour and cook this, then add the milk the mushrooms were cooked in, to make a sauce. Season with salt, pepper and a little paprika. Pour this sauce over the mushrooms and sprinkle it with the breadcrumbs and grated cheese. Put it in the oven to brown before serving. See also: Celery (and Mushroom Fry); Walnut (and Potato Pie).

NETTLES Fam. Urticaceae

Urtica dioica

Stinging nettles surely need little description. They grow profusely in waste places especially where there has been some cultivation. The young tops and shoots are the best part to eat. Wear gloves when coping with them!

CREAMED NETTLES

Nettle tops

Butter

Salt and pepper

Cream

Chives, shallots

or spring onions

Pick young nettle tops, wash them and strip off the leaves, and put them in a pan with a lump of butter and salt and pepper. Cook them slowly and stir them occasionally. When cooked and tender, strain off the liquid, then reheat the nettles with a little butter and some cream. A few chopped chives, shallots or spring onions cooked with the nettles will add flavour to the vegetable.

It is well worth while going to the little extra trouble of this recipe rather than just boiling the nettles for a few minutes before dishing them up. A child who had them to eat, badly served, described them to me as 'gritty, furry caterpillars'.

NETTLE SOUP 1

Nettle water

(see above recipe)

Béchamel sauce, or

cornflour, or

dehydrated potato

Save the juice from the above recipe combined with béchamel sauce; or add some cornflour or dehydrated potato and milk and butter. Leave a few finely-chopped pieces of nettle in the soup, and grate some cheese on top when serving.

NETTLE SOUP 2

1½ lb. nettles

1 lb. spinach

1 pt. beef stock

½ lb. frankfurters

2 tbsp. yoghurt

Wash the vegetables well. Blanch the nettles and mix them with the spinach. Pour the boiling stock over them and simmer for 40 minutes. Strain the stock and serve it with sliced frankfurters and yoghurt.

NETTLE FRITTERS

12 oz. young nettles	Breadcrumbs
1 egg	2 tbsp. grated cheese
Salt and pepper	Olive oil

Prepare the young nettles carefully and boil them in salted water until they are tender. Press out as much water as possible, then chop them finely; mix in the egg, salt and pepper and grated cheese. Divide the mixture into portions and roll them in the breadcrumbs. Fry them in deep olive oil.

NETTLE CHICKEN

Young chicken	Salt and pepper
Young nettles	Water
Oat or barley meal	Wild garlic or onion
Butter	or mint

This is a spring-time recipe for use when nettles are young and tender. Pick about $\frac{3}{4}$ pt. of nettles, wash them well in salted water and chop them small. Put the chicken into a heavy saucepan with 2 qts. of water. Bring it to the boil and add the nettles, a handful of oat or barley meal, salt, a knob of butter and some wild garlic. Simmer until the chicken is tender, and add more seasoning if necessary.

This is a Scottish recipe and traditionally the bird is first stuffed with the oatmeal or barley meal, and seasoned with salt, pepper and more wild garlic.

SPICED NETTLES AND POTATOES

2 lb. nettles	$\frac{1}{2}$ tspn. ground ginger
$\frac{1}{2}$ lb. potatoes	2 dry red chillis
2 oz. butter	1 tspn. cumin seed
1 large onion	Salt

Wash the nettles very thoroughly. Peel the potatoes and cut them in large dice. Heat the butter and fry the sliced onion until it is golden, then add the potatoes, cumin, chopped chillis and ginger. Cook them for 5 minutes, stirring all the time. Add the chopped nettles and cover the pan, having seasoned with salt. Cook gently until the mixture is fairly dry, and the nettles and potatoes are quite tender.

This recipe can be made with any other similar vegetable – sorrel, spinach, etc.

NETTLE COUNTRY PUDDING

6 handfuls young nettles	Sprig mint
1 handful dandelion	Thyme
leaves	1 onion
Small bunch watercress	Salt and pepper
Small bunch sorrel leaves	1 tbsp. butter
8 blackcurrant leaves	1 egg

Wash and chop the vegetables then mix them with all the other ingredients, put them in a basin, cover and steam them for 1½ hours. Serve very hot with rich brown gravy.

NETTLE WINE

2 qts. young nettle tops	2 lemons
3 lb. white sugar	½ oz. root ginger
1 gal. water	1 oz. yeast

Put the nettles and bruised ginger in a container and pour ⅔ of the boiling water over them, and mash. Leave it covered for 2 days, then make a syrup with the rest of the water and the sugar, and strain the liquid from the nettles into this. Add the juice of the lemons, and when cool, add the yeast and put the must into a fermentation jar. Finish as usual.

NETTLE BEER 1

2 lb. young nettles	2 lemons
1 gal. water	1 oz. cream of tartar
1 lb. demarara sugar	1 oz. yeast

Wash the nettles and boil them in the water for 15 minutes. Strain the liquid into a fermentation jar with the sugar, lemon peel without the pith, lemon juice, and cream of tartar. Stir, and when cool add the yeast. Cover the jar and leave it in a warm place for 3 days. Strain it and bottle it in screw topped cider or beer bottles. It will be ready to drink in about 8 days.

NETTLE BEER 2

2 qts. nettles	1 lb. sugar to each
1 pt. dandelions	gal. liquid
1 pt. currant leaves	1 tspn. cream of tartar
1 pt. goose grass	1 oz. yeast

Wash the nettles, currant leaves, goose grass and dandelions. Cover them with water and boil them quickly for 10 minutes. Strain the liquid through a sieve, on to the sugar, pressing hard to get all the juice. Stir thoroughly and when cool add the cream of tartar and the yeast. Allow this to ferment for a week. Rack, and leave to stand for another 2 days before bottling in strong screw-topped bottles. Drink within 3 weeks. See also: Sorrel (Turnovers – which can also be made with young nettles); and Fresh Spring Herb Soup (page 204).

OAK Fam. Fagaceae

Quercus robur

Oak trees are so familiar in this country that they need no description. Their only culinary use that I know of is as a flavouring for oak leaf wine which can be made throughout the summer and will be slightly different according to the age of the leaves.

OAK LEAF WINE

1 gal. oak leaves	3 lb. sugar
1 gal. water	$\frac{3}{4}$ oz. yeast
2 oranges	$\frac{1}{2}$ tspn, nutrient
1 lemon	

Pour the boiling water over the oak leaves, and after 24 hours strain the liquid on to the sugar and add the thin rind and juice of the oranges and lemons, and boil the lot together for 10 minutes. When cool, strain into fermentation jars, add the yeast and nutrient, and finish as usual.

PRIMROSE Fam. Primulaceae

Primula vulgaris

'Primmyrose Wine: After all worke done, mee ande Sarah toe thee woode toe pick primmy roses for thee wine maken, off wyche there bee grate store, wee getting 2 bagges full, then home agen to finde John verrie crosse att thee losse off another sowe, soe wee verrie carfulle nott toe crosse hym. I doe gett out a bottel of Eldernberrie wine and warme itt upp wythe a beaten egge and cinnamum off whyche hee bee verrie fonde, wych doe soone cure hys ill-hummor.

Then Sarah ande mee doe gett thee primmy roses reddie for thee wine, wych I doe always make sayme as mye dere mother didde. Thys is thee waye, off the primmy roses you doe take six measure from thee stolkes and crushe them in a wooden watt, then slyce upp 6 lemmons and laye on toppe, then sprinkel 2 handfuls of ginger in littel bittes, then another lott of primmy roses, lemons and ginger bittes, putt as well 6 styckes of cinnimun, shedd over over 2 punds of white sugar, ande add 6 pinte messures off colde boyled watter, leeve it till

nexte days, then stirr itt all uppe welle ande adde more colde
boyled watter toe cuvver over all, fasten over a clothe ande
leve itt 3 days, then stur everie day for a weke, taken care itt
bee the same hower eache daye, thenn adde 1 quarte messure
off brandie, sturringe all thee tyme. Nexte daye you doe putt in
6 punds off white sugger and stur till all bee melted, then
covver ande doe nott touche for another weke, after wyche
skimme off thee toppe skin ande strayne all twyce throughe
muslinn, and putte in another quarte messure of brandy. Putt
in a verrie clene drye caske and lett stande until noe more
frothe doe rise, then put in 2 clene egg shelles ande bunge
down tightlye for a yere, then putt in bottels reddie toe drynke.
Itt bee a fine drinke to use att a partie.'

The Diary of a Farmer's Wife, 18th April, 1796
Perhaps our best known wild flower, next to the bluebell, the
pale yellow primrose grows in woods and hedgerows and on
banks, and likes fairly moist conditions and some shade. Don't
overpick this flower as it is dying out for this reason in some
parts of the country.

CRYSTALLISED PRIMROSES
Primrose petals   water to 1 lb. sugar)
Syrup (approx 1 cup

Pick the primrose petals off their stalks. They must not be
damp. Boil the syrup to 'pearl' (approx 222°F. or 105°C. then
put the petals in and let it boil. Scoop the primroses out and
boil the sugar again until it begins to go white on the side of
the pan. Return the primroses to the syrup and reboil. Remove
the flowers, place them on a rack until they are completely
dry. Store them in airtight tins.

CANDIED PRIMROSES
Primroses   Water
Icing Sugar

Pick the primroses in dry weather and pull the petals away
from the green part. Make a syrup of icing sugar and water,
and boil it until a little dropped in cold water goes crisp. Then
put the petals in the syrup for a minute. Take them out and
drain them on a sieve. Leave them to dry fully in a warm

place, and when dry sprinkle them with a light dusting of icing sugar. Shake off the surplus, and store them in a dry place.

PRIMROSE WINE

1 gal. primrose flowers
1 gal. water
3 lb. white sugar
2 oranges

1 lemon
1 tspn. nutrient
¾ oz. yeast

Boil the water and stir in the sugar the thinly peeled rind of the fruit, the flowers, and fruit juice. When this is cool add the nutrient and yeast, and leave it covered for 5 days, stirring daily. Strain into fermentation jars, and continue as usual.

PUFFBALLS Fam. Calvatia

Calvatia caelata
Mosaic Puffball

Calvatia gigantea
Giant Puffball

The mosaic puffball is commoner in the north than in the south. It grows in grassy downs and meadows, and is pear-shaped, flattened at the top and as it grows the skin becomes cracked into hexagonal areas, raised in the centre. The giant puffball can grow to at least 1 ft. in diameter.

When puffballs are still young and fleshy, they can be sliced and fried, dipped in egg and breadcrumbs.

PUFFBALLS IN SAUCE

12 egg-sized puffballs	Cornflour
Flour	Bay leaf
Pepper and salt	Butter
Milk	Parsley
Onion	

Wipe the puffballs, then roll them in flour and pepper and salt, and put them in a bowl with just enough milk to cover them. Add a bay leaf and a little onion and simmer them gently until they are soft. Pour off the milk in which they were cooked, and thicken it with the butter and cornflour made into a roux. Season it as necessary and pour it back over the puffballs. Garnish with parsley.

RASPBERRY Fam. Rosaceae

Rubus idaeus

Extremely well known in its cultivated form, few people know that raspberries grow wild and are quite common. They like woods and heaths, and perhaps are mistaken for small unripe blackberries. The bushes do not grow anything like as vigorously as blackberry bushes, have woody stems on which the fruit grows, and small, less-vicious prickles than the blackberry. The easiest way to tell the difference is that the raspberry fruit, which is red when ripe, not black, comes easily off the bush, whereas a red unripe blackberry takes some shifting.

The fruit can be cooked by any recipe suitable for the cultivated fruit, but really nothing improves upon straight ripe raspberries and cream with a little castor sugar.

RASPBERRY CUSTARD

1 lb. raspberries
2 eggs
Knob of butter

3 oz. sugar
1 pt. milk

Grease a pie dish with the butter and put in the raspberries and sprinkle half the sugar over them. Beat the eggs, with the rest of the sugar and add the milk. Whisk again and pour this over the fruit. Bake it in a moderate oven until the top is golden brown.

RASPBERRY SOUFFLÉ

½ lb. raspberries
3 eggs
2 oz. cake crumbs
2 oz. white sugar

2 oz. cornflour
½ oz. butter
2 tbsp. cream

Beat the raspberries, cream, sugar and cornflour together until they form a pulp. Separate the yolks from the whites of the eggs. Beat the yolks and fold them into the raspberries, then add the cake crumbs. Whip the whites stiffly and fold them into the mixture. Bake in a hot oven in a soufflé dish for about ½ hour. Serve instantly.

POTTED RASPBERRIES

Raspberries
White sugar

Knob of butter

Use equal quantities of sugar and fruit. Warm the sugar in the oven, rub the butter round the preserving pan and put in the berries. When it bubbles, pour in the sugar. Stir with a wooden spoon for 30 minutes. Put into jars and seal.

RASPBERRY WINE

3 lb. ripe raspberries
3 lb. sugar
Juice of 1 lemon
1 tspn. nutrient

¾ oz. yeast
1 gal. water
1 Campden tablet

To make a beautiful 'Vin Rosé' pour the boiling water over the raspberries, and stir well. Add the Campden tablet and leave covered for 2 days, stiring frequently. Strain and squeeze the liquid on to the sugar and stir thoroughly; add the lemon juice and the nutrient and yeast, and put it all into a fermentation jar. Continue and finish as usual.

RASPBERRY RATAFIA

1 qt. raspberry	1 lb. sugar
juice	Pinch cinnamon
1 qt. brandy	Pinch cloves

Let the fruit juice stand in the fridge for 24 hours and then skim it. Mix it with the brandy, sugar and spices. Put it in a bottle and store it in the dark for a month, tightly corked, then strain and bottle it.

RASPBERRY LIQUEUR

2 qts. brandy	$\frac{1}{2}$ lb. sugar
1 lb. raspberries	Little water

Put some very ripe raspberries in a jar with the brandy. Seal the jar and leave it to infuse for 2 months, in as much sunshine as possible. Add to it the sugar dissolved in a very little water. Mix it all well, strain carefully, and bottle.

See also: Cottage Cheese with Strawberries (page 188), which can be made with raspberries; and Summer Pudding (page 105).

ROSE WILD Fam. Rosaceae

Rosehips are the fruit of the English wild rose or dog rose and are the part of the plant used in cooking. They came into great favour during World War II for their high vitamin C content, and have remained a favourite source of supply of this vitamin. The bush grows in hedgerows and in waste places in the south. Sweetbriar, smaller and sweet smelling with sticky undersides to its leaves, is fairly common on chalk and limestone in the south. In the north, the downy rose is more common. It has pinker flowers, and rounder hips covered with bristles.

Hips should be left on the bushes until the frost has touched

Rosa canina
Dog Rose

R. rubiginosa
Sweetbriar

R. villosa
Downy Rose

them and they become slightly soft. If you do not want to dry them, they can be picked a little earlier, but not before October. They can be made into purée, or syrups, sauces, creams, puddings or soups. Use fresh rosehips.

If the hips are to be dried and crushed, do not let them come into contact with metal, other than stainless steel, as it makes the hips black, and they lose vitamin C.

Rose petals can be crystallised for decoration (see page 194).

To make rose vinegar, put a few rose petals into a mild wine vinegar and leave them there for several days.

ROSE HIP CREAM

½ pt. prepared rose   1½ pts. water
  hips   3 tbsp. cornflour
¼ lb. sugar

Make sure the hips are ripe and red. Split them, and remove all the seeds and small hairs. Rinse them and put them in water and boil them gently until they are soft, stirring occasionally. Put the mixture through a sieve or blender and boil the purée with the sugar. Remove the scum. Mix the cornflour with a little water to a thin cream, and pour it into the rose hip syrup, boil again and pour it into moulds or a basin. Serve it chilled with plenty of cream.

ROSE HIP AND APPLE JAM

1 lb. rose hips   1 lb. apples
¾ lb. sugar   Water

Cover the rose hips with the water and simmer for 2 hours. Strain the juice through a jelly bag overnight. Next day slice up the prepared apples and cook them until they are a pulp. Add the sugar and rose hip juice and boil them for ½ hour or until they are set. Put the jelly in jars and seal them.

ROSE HIP TEA 1

2 tbsp. rose hips   3 pts. water

Soak the rose hips (equal amount of pips and pods) in the water for 12 hours. Or pour the 3 pints of boiling water over them. Simmer gently for ½ hour, strain and keep covered in a china or earthenware jar until they are needed. A few extra hips can be added each time when reheated. Sweeten the tea with brown sugar or honey.

ROSE HIP TEA 2

¾ oz. rose hip pips   1¾ pts. water

Pour the cold water over the seeds, and bring them to the boil. Simmer gently for about ¾ hour, then strain.

ROSE HIP WINE

1 gal. ripe rose hips	Campden tablet
1 gal. water	1 tspn. nutrient
2¾ lb. sugar	¾ oz. yeast
1 lemon, 1 orange	1 tspn. pectozyme

Wash the berries and crush them well before pouring boiling water over them, Use non-metal containers and equipment. When they are cool add the thinly peeled rind of the fruit and the juice, the campden tablet and the pectozyme. Leave for 24 hours, stirring occasionally. Strain and squeeze the liquid on to the sugar. Stir until it is dissolved, add the nutrient and yeast, and put it all into a fermentation jar. Continue and finish as usual.

See also: Blackberry (Bramble and Rose Hip Jam).

Rowan Fam. Rosaceae

Sorbus aucuparia
Mountain Ash

A common, neat-looking tree, which grows in dry woods and mountains, and occasionally in hedgerows. It has smooth grey bark, and large, alternate pinnate leaves. The flowers grow in flattish white heads and smell unpleasant, but turn to clusters of brilliant red berries. It is these berries which are cooked.

ROWAN JELLY

2 lb. rowan berries	1½ lb. sugar
¾ pt. water	Lemon juice

Stalk the berries and wash and drain them. Put them into a preserving pan with 2 tablespoons of lemon juice and the water. Simmer until they are soft, then put them in a jelly bag and leave them overnight. Measure the juice and put 1 lb. of sugar to each pint of juice. Put these into a pan and boil them until they are set. Pour the jelly into jars and seal them.

This jelly can also be made by using an equal quantity of apple or crab apple juice instead of lemon juice, and once again sugar is added at 1 lb. to 1 pt. of juice.

Rowan jelly is particularly good with grouse, venison or lamb.

SALISFY Fam. Compositae

Tragopogon porrifolius
Salisfy

T. pratensis
Goatsbeard

Wild salisfy is not very common and grows near the sea or in waste places. It has narrow, greyish leaves rather like grass, but fleshier, which sheath the stems. These stems swell out under the flower heads which have narrow bracts enclosing dull purple, dandelion-like flowers. The tap root is used as a vegetable.

Goatsbeard is much the same, but has yellow flowers which

only open in the morning, and less swollen stems beneath the flower heads, and is much more common, growing in damp and rich pastureland.

The young shoots of both can be eaten in salads, prepared like spinach, or the roots of salisfy are cooked and eaten in various ways. The plant is cultivated for its tap root.

BOILED SALISFY

Salisfy	Lemon juice or
Court bouillon	vinegar

Scrape the roots, divide them in pieces about 3 in. long and cook them in water with a little lemon juice or vinegar to stop them turning black. Cook covered with court bouillon gently for 1 hour. Drain them well before serving.

SALISFY IN SAUCE

Salisfy	Parmesan cheese
Mornay sauce	Butter

Stew the prepared salisfy roots in butter, put them in a dish lined with a layer of mornay sauce and sprinkle a little grated parmesan cheese on top. Pour over some melted butter, and brown it in the oven or under the grill.

SALISFY SALAD

Salisfy	Vinegar (or lemon
Olive oil	juice)
Court bouillon	Chopped parsley,
Salt and pepper	chervil and tarragon

Cook the cleaned salisfy in a flour and water court bouillon. Drain it, dry and cut it in small pieces. Put the bits in a bowl, and season them with the oil, vinegar, salt and pepper, chopped parsley, chervil and tarragon.

SAUTÉED SALISFY

Salisfy	Parsley
Equal amounts of	Pressed garlic
butter and olive oil	

Sauté the prepared salisfy in the butter and oil, and just before serving, add a tablespoonful of chopped parsley and garlic.

SALISFY FRITTERS

Salisfy	1 tbsp. flour
Egg	Fat for frying

Clean, slice and cook the salisfy until it is tender. Beat up the egg and flour. Pulp the salisfy and stir it into the egg and flour mixture to make it the consistency of thin batter. Drop a large spoonful at a time in boiling fat and fry it.

SAMPHIRE Fam. Umbelliferae/Fam. Salicornia

Crithmum maritimum
Peter's Cress, Sea Fennel

Salicornia herbacea
Marsh Samphire,
Glasswort

Samphire grows on sea cliffs and is only common locally. The plant grows to about 1 ft. high, and is rather grey looking. It has thick fleshy leaves and solid stems. The smell is not unlike salty, oily celery, if that is descriptive enough!

Where it grows, glasswort is known as marsh samphire, and is cooked and eaten as such. It appears in great bright green meadows in salt marshes, from July on. It has cylindrical branched and segmented spikes of fleshy green, and when cooked the fleshy part strips off the thin woody skeleton of the plant. When harvesting, cut the plants off carefully leaving behind as much mud as possible.

True samphire is eaten usually in a salad or pickled in vinegar, like gherkins.

PICKLED SAMPHIRE

Samphire	Chillis
Vinegar	Sprig of thyme
Small white onions	Cloves
Salt	

Clean and trim the samphire and soak it for 24 hours. Drain, and wipe it well with a cloth. Put the samphire in a large bowl, covered with vinegar which has been boiled. Leave it to steep for 10 hours. Drain off the vinegar, re-boil it with more fresh vinegar, allowing $\frac{1}{2}$ pt. fresh to every 3 pts. of boiled vinegar. Pour all this boiling vinegar over the samphire. Drain the samphire after a few minutes, put it in jars with some small white onions, a few chillis, a sprig of thyme, some cloves, and cover these all again with the vinegar. Seal the jars carefully.

SAMPHIRE IN CREAM

Samphire	Salt and pepper
Water	Cream
Butter	

Boil the samphire in salted water until it is just tender. Drain and dry it in a cloth. Return it to the pan and then toss the samphire in a little melted butter for a few seconds. Then add thick cream and simmer until the sauce has been reduced to half its original volume. Season and serve very hot.

BUTTERED SAMPHIRE

Marsh samphire	Salt and pepper
Water	Butter

Wash the plants thoroughly in several rinses of cold water. Put them in a saucepan and cover with water. Boil them for 20 minutes until the fleshy part slips easily off the stalks. Drain them, season with salt and pepper and serve piping hot with melted butter.

Eat the samphire by picking up each piece and sucking it. A hot-plate is useful when serving it, because samphire takes time to eat and gets cold rather quickly.

It is equally tasty eaten cold dipped in home-made mayonnaise (see page 36), or sprinkled with a little lemon juice, oil and vinegar.

SEAKALE Fam. Cruciferae

Crambe maritima

Grows on sea shores and cliffs and is a kind of cabbage with white, sweet scented flowers, rather like a bolted cauliflower.

SEAKALE IN SAUCE

Seakale   Salt and pepper
Béchamel sauce

Trim the white ribs to about the size of a finger. Boil them until tender. Put the cooked green parts of the vegetable through a sieve, and season with salt and pepper. Arrange the white seakale ribs in the centre of a dish with the green puréed leaves round them, and pour about $\frac{1}{2}$ pt. of sauce over the lot.

SILVERWEED Fam. Rosaceae

Potentilla anserina

This is a creeping plant with toothed silvery leaves and single yellow flowers on long stalks. It is quite unmistakable when its pinnate, fern-like leaves grow profusely on freshly cultivated ground, and in damp, grassy waste places. No other creeping silver coloured plant has yellow flowers.

The roots of the silverweed for the following recipe must be collected in March and April when they are fairly young, being long, thin and white or cream coloured. They are easiest to find and pull up in a recently cultivated field.

SILVERWEED BANNOCKS

Silverweed roots	Salt
Water	Butter
Oatmeal or barley meal	Milk

Wash and rinse the roots carefully in cold water, and scrape them if necessary. Spread them out to dry completely in the sun. When they are dry and brittle, break them into tiny pieces, put them in a cloth, tie it tightly and pound with a pestle until reduced to a powder. Or put them in a coffee grinder and reduce them to a powder that way. Mix the powder with oatmeal or barley meal and a pinch of salt, then rub in a pat of butter. Make a hole in the centre and pour in, very slowly, enough milk to make a stiff paste. Roll it into a round about ½ in. thick. Heat a bannock slab in front of the fire, then turn it and toast the other side. If you do not have a bannock slab (or an open fire) toast the bannock in a *very* heavy iron pan on the top of the stove, and turn it over to toast the other side. Do not put fat in the pan, but keep it dry and take care it does not burn.

SNOWDROP Fam. Amaryllidaceae

Galanthus nivalis

So well known because it is the first flower of the year, blooming February, March, when it appears in woods and damp places, even pushing up through snow. The plant is fairly common wild in England, although it is usually an escape.

SNOWDROP WINE

2½ pts. snowdrop   3 lb. sugar
  flowers   ½ lb. raisins
1 gal. water   ¾ oz. yeast
1 lb. rice

Boil the snowdrops in the water for 10 minutes, add the rice and boil for a further 10 minutes. Strain the liquid over the sugar and raisins. When cool, add the yeast and put the lot in a fermentation jar. After 10 days strain off the liquid into another jar, leaving behind the raisins and sediment. Ferment to a finish.

SOLOMON'S SEAL Fam. Liliaceae

Polygonatum multiflorum

Not very common, but where it is found Solomon's seal grows in some profusion. The plant is similar to the one found cultivated in gardens. Purplish shoots appear in the spring, and it is these that can be eaten, prepared like asparagus. As the shoots open up they become arching stems with broad elliptical leaves, from which hang clusters of greenish-white unscented flowers like little bells.

SORREL Fam. Polygonaceae

Rumex acetosa

Sorrel is a common member of the dock family, and grows about 2 ft. high in waste places. The leaves are arrow-shaped and on long stalks, except for the upper leaves which sheath the stem. The long flower spikes are green and turn brown as they ripen to little round fruits.

Sorrel leaves have a slightly bitter flavour and are excellent when mixed with spinach, lettuce or cabbage. The French use them as a vegetable mixed with the above in the same way as the English use spinach. They also use them for sorrel soup. Young sorrel leaves are good in lettuce salads or chopped into egg and dish dishes. When used to garnish fish dishes, mix them with chopped parsley, tarragon and chives, but use twice as much sorrel as the other herbs.

Add a handful of chopped sorrel to lentil soup, or tomato soup, about 5 minutes before serving.

Cook sorrel for as short a time as possible to retain the flavour and cut it only with a stainless steel knife, as it reacts with iron to make a metallic taste and nasty black stains.

Sorrel leaves can be bottled by cooking them, then putting them into Kilner jars and treating and sterilising them in the usual way (see page 31).

SORREL PUREE

1 lb. sorrel	5 tbsp. butter
1 cup water	Salt
Roux (flour, butter, white stock)	Castor sugar
	$\frac{1}{4}$ cup cream
3 egg yolks	

Wash the sorrel several times, and put it into a saucepan with the water. Cook slowly until the water is reduced. Drain the sorrel and put it into a casserole which contains the roux made with 2 tbsp. butter, 1 tbsp. flour and $1\frac{1}{2}$ cups white stock. Season this with salt and a little sugar, cover the dish and cook in a moderate oven for 2 hours. Rub the sorrel through a sieve or put it in a blender, and reheat it. Then add 3 egg yolks mixed with the cream, blended with the butter. Stir well, and serve with veal, pork, fish or omelettes.

SHREDDED SORREL

Sorrel   Butter
Water

Shred the sorrel very finely indeed, having washed it. Simmer it gently in a little butter, until the water in the sorrel has evaporated.

SORREL OMELETTE

Eggs   Butter
Shredded sorrel   Salt and pepper

Add 4 tbsp. of shredded sorrel to the eggs while they are being beaten, and make the omelette in the usual way.

COLD SORREL SOUP

1 lb. sorrel leaves   1 tbsp. chopped celery
3 pts. chicken stock   Salt and pepper
3 tbsp. sugar   2 hard boiled eggs
$\frac{3}{4}$ oz. chopped parsley   1 cup sour cream or
2 tbsp. lemon juice   yoghurt

Cook the sorrel leaves, parsley and celery in the stock for 45 minutes. Add the lemon juice, sugar and salt and pepper. Put the soup into a bowl in the fridge and when it is quite cold, stir in the sour cream or yoghurt, and garnish with slices of hard boiled egg.

SORREL AND CHERVIL SOUP

$\frac{1}{2}$ lb. sorrel   2 tbsp. butter
Chervil to taste   1 cup cream
2 slices bread   Salt and pepper
2 pints water

Take the stalks from the sorrel and chervil, wash the leaves well, and chop them. Fry them in butter, add the seasoned water and simmer for $\frac{1}{2}$ hour. Crumble the bread and add it to the soup. Before serving put a bit more bread in each bowl, and stir in a little cream, and freshly ground black pepper.

SORREL AND KIDNEYS

Sorrel   Cayenne
Kidneys   Butter
Salt and pepper   Nutmeg

Slice as many kidneys as required and season them with salt, pepper and cayenne, and fry them in butter. Prepare a purée of sorrel, add pepper, salt and nutmeg. Serve it very hot with the sorrel in the middle of the dish, and the kidneys poured round the edge.

SORREL TURNOVERS

2 cups sorrel	2½ cups flour
Handful walnuts	Cayenne pepper
1 onion	Salt
3 tbsp. olive oil	Fat for frying

Wash the sorrel and chop it and mix it with the minced onion, seasoning, about half the oil, chopped walnuts and lemon juice. Mix the flour with the rest of the olive oil, a little salt and enough water to make a dough. Roll this out into convenient sized pieces and fill with the sorrel mixture. Close up the dough round it, and fry the turnovers in hot fat until they are brown.

See also: Nettles (Country Pudding; and Spiced Nettles and Potatoes).

Sow THISTLE Fam. Compositae

Sonchus oleraceus

Swine's Thistle, Hare's Lettuce, Milkweed, Milky Dickle.

This plant grows up to 3 ft. high and is grey-green with flower heads of small pale yellow dandelion type. The stem, when broken, exudes milky juice. The dull leaves sheath the stem loosely and are arrow-shaped. The lower leaves are irregularly pinnate and toothed.

The tender leaves in spring can be used in salads.

In winter the roots are eaten. Prepare them the same way as salisfy.

BUTTERED SOW THISTLE

Young sow thistle leaves	Chopped chives or spring onions
Butter	Lemon juice
Salt and pepper	

Wash the young leaves and put them still wet into a pan with a good knob of butter and cook them slowly. Stir to prevent them burning. Season with salt and pepper. The flavour is improved by the addition of chopped chives or spring onions. Serve with a squeeze of lemon juice.

Many edible weeds can be cooked and eaten as a mixture, dandelions and sow-thistles combining particularly well.

STRAWBERRY (WILD) Fam. Rosaceae

Fragaria vesca

'Doubtless God could have made a better berry, but doubtless God never did.'   William Butler, quoted by
Isaak Walton, *The Compleat Angler.*

Wild strawberries grow in open woods and grassy banks, and are just smaller versions of the cultivated plant, with creeping green trefoil leaves and little white flowers. The leaves are bright green above, paler beneath, with little hairs.

Wild strawberries have a marvellous sharp flavour, and can be cooked, if you have enough, by any method appropriate to cultivated strawberries. But eaten as they are, with fresh cream and castor sugar, they take a lot of beating. Champagne and wild strawberries go exceptionally well together.

COTTAGE CHEESE WITH STRAWBERRIES

8 oz. cottage cheese	Sugar to taste
8 oz. strawberries	Lemon juice

Wash the strawberries. Rub the cottage cheese then the strawberries through a fine sieve or put it through a blender. Season with lemon juice and sugar. Whisk the mixture until it is creamy, and serve decorated with a few whole strawberries.

STRAWBERRIES, ICE CREAM AND KIRSCH

$\frac{1}{2}$ lb. strawberries	1 tbsp. Kirsch (or
Large cupful ice	sherry)
cream	2 oz. sugar

Put the strawberries in a bowl and pour the kirsch over them. Sprinkle with sugar, stir in the ice cream, and enjoy it!

STRAWBERRIES IN CHAMPAGNE

4 cups wild strawberries	$\frac{1}{4}$ cup blanched toasted
1 cup champagne (or	almonds
sparkling home made	2 cups cream
wine)	4 tbsp. cherry brandy
$\frac{3}{4}$ cup sugar	

Put the prepared strawberries in a bowl and sprinkle them with sugar. Add half the cherry brandy (home-made will do very well indeed) and all the champagne. Put this in the fridge until it is very cold. Add the remaining cherry brandy to the well-whipped cream, put it on the strawberries, and decorate with the almonds.

STRAWBERRY JAM

Strawberries	Sugar

Put equal weights of sugar and strawberries in a preserving pan. Stir them gently until the berries are coated with sugar. Leave them for 24 hours, then bring them to the boil. After 3 or 4 minutes scoop out the berries with a sieve and put them into warmed jars. Reheat the syrup and boil it until it is set (220°F. or 105°C.). Pour this over the fruit, and seal the jars in the usual way.

STRAWBERRY JELLY

2½ pts. strawberries   1 lemon
½ lb. sugar   1 pt. water

Put the strawberries, lemon juice and water in a preserving pan. Bring them to the boil and simmer until all the juice is extracted. Strain and measure the juice. Add the sugar and boil it until the jelly is set. Skim, pot and seal.

STRAWBERRY WINE

1 gal. strawberries   1 lemon
3 lb. sugar   1 tspn. nutrient
1 gal. water   ¾ oz. yeast

Pour boiling water on to the fruit and mash it well. Leave it to stand for 2 days and then strain and squeeze the juice over the sugar. Add the lemon juice and other ingredients, stir well, and pour it into a fermentation jar. Add ½ lb. raisins to the strawberries in the first operation to produce a heavier wine. Without the raisins, the wine will be light, delicately coloured and flavoured, and fairly sweet.

See also: Summer Pudding (page 105); Woodruff (Cup); and Metheglin (page 207).

SWEET CECILY Fam. Umbelliferae

This plant looks rather like common cow parsley, but is bigger and longer with white umbels of flowers on stalks 3–4 ft. high. It often has small white flecks on the leaves. Most characteristic is the definite aniseed smell when crushed. It is rare in southern England, but quite common in the north, and southern and central Scotland. It is very often found near houses as it is usually an escape, having for years been cultivated for its herbal uses.

Myrrhis odorata
Sweet Chervil

Sweet Cecily has a sweetish aniseed flavour. Use the leaves and crushed seeds in drinks, fruit cups, fruit salads, stewed tart fruit like rhubarb, gooseberry, currants, plums, damsons, etc., to remove some of the sharpness, only about half the usual amount of sugar having to be added. The fresh chopped leaves can be used in salads, soups, fish and with root vegetables, as well as with sugared strawberries, or as a green topping to the whipped cream. It can be mixed in trifles, raw vegetable juices, slimming cocktails, omelettes, pancakes and herb butter.

The tap root can be boiled, and then sliced and dressed with oil and vinegar to make an unusual addition to a salad.

GOOSEBERRY TART WITH SWEET CECILY AND BALM
1 lb. unripe gooseberries   1 tspn. lemon balm
2 to 3 tspn. sweet   2 oz. sugar
  cecily   Pastry

Line a tin with pastry. Boil the gooseberries, herbs and sugar in a little water until they are tender. Scoop out the gooseberries and pack them in the pastry case, cover it with more pastry, and bake in the oven in the usual way.
See also: Bilberry (Soup).

Tansy Fam. Compositae

Tanacetum vulgare

This plant grows to 3 ft. tall, on grassy waste ground. The leaves are fern-like and the flowers are neat, big clusters of little yellow buttons.

The flavour is strong and the taste an acquired one, but in the past tansy was used to flavour custards, milk puddings and cakes; a chopped tansy leaf or two being added while cooking. It is also sometimes used as an ingredient of stuffing for omelettes and fresh water fish.

'Minnow Tansies: The minnows are washed well in salt, and their heads and tails cut off, and their guts taken out, and not washed after, they prove excellent for that use; that is being fried with yolk of eggs, the flowers of cowslips and of primroses, and a little tansy; thus they make a dainty dish of meat.'

Izaak Walton, *The Compleat Angler*

TANSY WINE

1 large handful tansy
    leaves and flowers
1 lemon
1 gal. water
4 lb. parsnips

3 lb. sugar
¼ pt. cold tea
1 tspn. nutrient
¾ oz. yeast

Basically parsnip wine flavoured with tansy. Scrub and slice the parsnips and cook them until tender. Strain the liquid over the sugar. Infuse the tansy for an hour in enough boiling water to cover and add this to the other liquid with the lemon juice and cold tea. When cool add the nutrient and yeast and pour the must into a fermentation jar. Finish as usual.

THYME Fam. Labiatae

Thymus drucei

'Who has not experienced the virtues of thyme and Pennyroyal?'
        Alexander Neckham, (trans.) *De Rerum Naturalis*, 1157.

Thyme forms mats of dark green small leaves on woody stems, with little purple flowers. It is common on dry grassy heaths and downs, sometimes on dunes, but is only found on downlands in the south east. It is recognisable by its unmistakable smell.

Thyme has a clove-like flavour which can overpower more delicate herbs if used too liberally. It is good with mutton or pork, eels and shellfish. It is an almost essential ingredient in meat stews and casserole dishes, especially when blended with wine, onion, garlic and brandy.

Add ½ tspn. of thyme to cottage and cream cheeses. Thyme can also be added to tomato juice, fish and seafood, sauerkraut juice, mixed raw vegetable juice, crab, mussels, all raw salads, scrambled and baked eggs, pancakes, cheese sauce, all vegetable soups; rub it on beef, lamb, pork and veal before cooking; put it in gravy, sausages, fish, chicken, turkey, and stuffings for all poultry and game, and also with mushrooms, beans, carrots, and aubergines.

See also: Chestnuts (Freshwater Fish Stuffed with); Garlic (Soup); Samphire (Pickled); and Herb Wine (page 206).

VIOLETS Fam. Violaceae

Viola odorata

'... I hope you have a good store of double violets – I think they are the Princesses of flowers, and in a shower of rain, almost as fine as barley sugar drops are to a schoolboy's tongue.'   John Keats, 1819.

There are several species of wild violet, but only one smells really sweet. The heart-shaped, downy leaves and violet flowers, (sometimes white, pink or yellow) grow in tufts directly from the bases of the plants. Common in hedges and shady places. They flower in spring and sometimes again in the autumn.

Candied violet petals are used in pastry making, confectionery, the making of ices and iced mousses, and in the preparation of salads.

VIOLET SALAD

Violet leaves and flowers
Celery
Endive
Parsley
Olive oil
Salt and pepper
Wine vinegar or lemon juice

Make a salad with all the ingredients mixed well together.

G

VIOLET SOUFFLÉ

½ cup candied violets	2 tbsp. sugar
2 tbsp. butter	3 egg yolks, 4 egg
1 cup hot milk	whites
2 tbsp. flour	1 tbsp. Kümmel

Melt the butter and add the flour, stirring all the time. Pour in the hot milk slowly and boil until thickened. Remove it from the heat and cool it to lukewarm. Add the sugar, Kümmel and the egg yolks, mixing well after each egg yolk has gone in. Beat the egg whites and fold them in. Add the candied violets, broken in 2 or 3 pieces each. Decorate the top of the soufflé with more violets when it has been put into the soufflé dish. Cook in a pre-heated moderate oven for 20 minutes and serve the soufflé instantly.

CRYSTALLISED VIOLETS

Violet petals	of water to 1 lb.
Syrup (approx. 1 cup	sugar

Pick the violet petals as dry as possible, and cut the heads from the stems. Boil the syrup to 'pearl' (222°F. or 105°C.), then put the violets in and let it reboil. Scoop the flowers out and boil the sugar again until it begins to get white on the side of the pan. Put the violets back in the syrup and reboil. Take out the violets, place them on a rack to dry completely. Store them in airtight tins until needed.

The same recipe can be used for cowslips, primroses and roses.

VIOLET SYRUP

½ lb. violets	1½ lb. sugar
1 pt. water	

Cut the flower heads off the stalks and put them in a bowl. Pour the boiling water over them and let them steep for about 12 hours. Sieve the liquid and add the sugar, stirring it well till it is dissolved. Bring the sugar and violet liquid to the boil, then take it off the heat straight away. Leave it in the saucepan with the lid on until it is nearly cold, then bottle it.

VIOLET LIQUEUR

1 pt. brandy	1 cup sugar
¼ lb. violets	¼ tspn. cinnamon
1 clove	1 cup water

Put the violet petals in the alcohol with the clove and cinnamon for 1 month. Strain off the liquid and add a syrup made from the sugar and water. Mix it well and bottle it.

VIOLET SHRUB (Old recipe)

Violets	Wine
Honey	

Soak some violet petals in wine for a week. Strain out the petals, and put some more fresh ones in for another week. Strain and bottle the wine, and add a little honey when serving it.

WALNUT Fam. Juglandaceae

Juglans regia

The walnut is not native to Britain, but grows readily here, and in the past many thousands were planted, for their stately beauty, for their fine wood and for their nuts. Although perhaps the greater proportion of them have now been cut down as the timber is so valuable, small walnut trees still abound in gardens and a few can be found wild. The nuts are encased in smooth, slightly knobbly green husks, which stain the hands brown when broken. When the nuts are ripe, the inside shell is woody and hard, but when used for pickling the nuts must be gathered before the inside shell has hardened. When they are like this, they are known as green walnuts. The fleshy casing is called the shuck.

Fresh walnuts are good to eat and dried walnuts are mainly used in cookery, although they are more difficult to digest because of their high fat content.

PICKLED WALNUTS 1

Green walnuts	Peppercorns
Vinegar	Whole ginger
Salt	Cloves
Allspice	

Wipe the walnuts with a dry cloth. Put them in Kilner jars and cover them with vinegar. Seal the jars and leave them to stand in a cool dry place for 4 months. Drain off the vinegar and boil as much fresh vinegar as will cover the walnuts with the seasonings in the following proportions. To each 3 pts. of vinegar allow 1 oz. salt, and $\frac{1}{2}$ oz. each of allspice, peppercorns, cloves and whole ginger. Pour all this over the walnuts while it is boiling hot. Cover carefully and store in a cool dry place. Wait for 3 weeks before using any of the pickled walnuts.

PICKLED WALNUTS 2

Walnuts	Brine (1 lb. salt to
Spiced vinegar	1 gal. water)

Pick the green walnuts in early July. If a needle, pushed into the shells, goes in easily, they are right for pickling by this method. Prick the walnuts with a fork and leave them in the brine for a week. Drain them and put them on old dishes that will not hurt if they are stained, and leave them in the sunshine, or bright light, for about 2 days. Turn them once or twice until the nuts are black all over. Pack them into jars, cover them with cold spiced vinegar, and seal the jars well.

WALNUT KETCHUP

4 lb. green walnut shells	$\frac{1}{2}$ cup cayenne pepper
2 lb. rock salt	$\frac{3}{4}$ cup powdered spice
$\frac{3}{4}$ cup ginger	$\frac{1}{2}$ cup cloves

Put the walnut shells and rock salt in a large bowl and leave them for 6 days. Crush the shells several times with a pestle.

Leave the bowl slightly tilted after each crushing so that the juice can be poured off easily. When all the juice has gone, and just the pulp remains, boil the juice and skim it. Add to the skimmed juice the ginger, spice, cayenne pepper and cloves. Simmer these for $\frac{1}{2}$ hour and pour into small bottles. Store in a dry place. Leave for some months before using.

WALNUT AND GARLIC SAUCE

3 lb. skinned walnuts   5 oz. olive oil
3 cloves garlic   Salt to taste

Pound or grind the walnuts with the garlic, and season with salt. Then add, very slowly indeed, the olive oil, stirring all the time until it becomes a thick sauce. This sauce is very good as an hors-d'œuvre with bread, or as a raw celery dip. It is also nice with cold meat.

POTATO AND WALNUT PANCAKES

4 oz. chopped walnuts   4 eggs
2 lb. cooked potatoes   2 tbsp. olive oil
2 oz. chopped suet   Salt and pepper

Melt the suet in a heavy frying pan. Add the oil, and when very hot add the mashed potatoes, eggs, chopped walnuts and salt and pepper. Fry into one huge pancake until golden on both sides. Garnish it before serving with a few more walnuts, and a little chopped parsley or lettuce.

WALNUT AND POTATOE PIE

$\frac{1}{4}$ lb. shelled walnuts   Mushroom ketchup
1 lb. mashed potato   Butter
$\frac{1}{2}$ pt. stock   Salt and pepper

Butter a pie-dish, put in a layer of potato, pepper and salt. Chop the walnuts finely and cover the potatoes with them. Pour over the stock and some mushroom ketchup (see recipe on page 159) to taste. Bake in a moderate oven for $\frac{1}{2}$ hour.

WALNUT PUDDING

6 oz. shelled walnuts   5 eggs
6 oz. castor sugar   Powdered cinnamon

Grind the walnuts and flavour them with a pinch of cinnamon. Beat the egg yolks with the sugar and beat in the ground walnuts. Whisk the egg whites stiffly and fold them in. Put the mixture into a greased bowl covered with greaseproof paper. Steam it for 1 hour. When it is cold, turn it out of the basin, and eat it cold with whipped cream.

WALNUT FUDGE

$\frac{1}{4}$ lb. chopped walnuts
1 lb. brown sugar
1 tbsp. golden syrup
$\frac{1}{2}$ pt. thin cream
$\frac{1}{2}$ tspn. vanilla essence

Put the sugar, cream and syrup into a saucepan, and stir it while it comes to the boil. Boil it for 15 to 20 minutes. Take it off the heat, stir in the walnuts and vanilla, put the saucepan in a bowl of cold water until the liquid thickens. Pour it into a buttered tin, and leave it to set.

WALNUT LIQUEUR 1

20 green walnuts
1 lb. sugar
$1\frac{1}{2}$ qts. brandy
1 cup boiled water
Cinnamon
Coriander

Split the green walnuts in half and put them in a jar with the brandy for 6 weeks in a cool place. Shake the jar occasionally. Strain the liquid off and make a syrup from the sugar and water and add that and a pinch of cinnamon and coriander. Leave this to infuse for a month, then bottle.

WALNUT LIQUEUR 2

100 green walnuts
$1\frac{1}{2}$ qts. brandy
1 cup boiled water
4 lb. sugar
$\frac{1}{2}$ tbsp. cloves

Use unripe nuts and prick them with a pin. Then proceed as in the above recipe, but leave it to infuse for the first period for 2 months.

WATERCRESS Fam. Cruciferae

A hairless perennial which grows in shallow fresh water, particularly chalk streams, but also colonises on muddy stream

Nasturtium officinale

bottoms. It has roundish, dark green or brownish shiny leaves, and white flowers. Characterised by its special taste, it grows plentifully wild, but do be sure that the stream in which you find it is clean, and always wash the cress very thoroughly indeed before using it.

Watercress is usually eaten raw in salads, or as garnish on meat, etc. For salads it should be trimmed and washed, dried and seasoned with olive oil, vinegar (or lemon juice) and salt and pepper.

WATERCRESS SOUP 1
1 lb. watercress	Butter
Roux (flour, butter, milk or stock)	Cream

Blanch, press and chop the watercress, then cook it in butter. Add the roux. The amount depends on how many servings, but for 1 lb. of watercress you will need about ¾ pt. milk. If it is a little thick, more milk can be added. Put the watercress through a sieve or blender, or else leave it in the soup in finely chopped pieces. Just before serving, add 2 tbsp. of cream.

WATERCRESS SOUP 2

2 large bunches of watercress	Cream
	Butter
Water	3 potatoes
Milk	2 egg yolks

Wash, chop and dry the watercress then cook it for a few minutes in 1½ oz. butter. Add the water then the peeled and diced potatoes. Boil these for 25 minutes. Sieve or put it through a blender, and add enough milk to make the right consistency, simmer again, and just before serving, add the egg yolks and a little cream. Garnish the soup with chopped watercress.

WATERCRESS SANDWICH

Watercress	Salt and paprika
Butter	Caviare
Toast	Lemon juice

Chop the watercress very finely indeed and mix it to a paste with the butter. Spread it on the toast. Sprinkle it with salt and paprika, and cover it with caviare seasoned with lemon juice!

WATERCRESS CREAM

Watercress	Salt
Water	Cream

Cook the washed, trimmed watercress in boiling salted water, drain it, dry it, and add a few tablespoons of fresh boiling cream. Butter can be used instead of cream.
See also: Nettle (Country Pudding); Herb Butter (page 203); Herb Mayonnaise (page 204).

WOODRUFF Fam. Rubiaceae

A delicate little plant growing up to 1 ft. high. The slightly shiny leaves grow in whorls spaced apart up the single stems. It has little white heads of flowers. Woodruff grows everywhere in moist woods mainly on chalk and limestone. It smells of new mown hay when crushed.

Galium odoratum

The German name for this plant means 'master of the woods' and people gather it in Germany and steep it in dry white wine to impart flavour. The French use woodruff with champagne, the Swiss serve Benedictine and Cognac impregnated with woodruff. It is also delicious if used with fruit drinks, and clear apple juice flavoured with woodruff is one of the nicest fruit drinks.

WOODRUFF TEA
Infuse or steep the leaves in the usual way, or add a sprig of the dried herb to ordinary China tea.

WOODRUFF CUP
1 bottle white wine
Woodruff leaves
Lemon rind and juice
Sugar

Strawberries or
   peaches
Soda water or champagne

Put the woodruff with ⅓ of a bottle of wine and let it steep for 1 hour. Filter, or strain this through a fine muslin cloth, and add it to the rest of the wine, the grated lemon rind and juice, the strawberries or peaches, and add sugar to taste. Pour soda water (or preferably champagne) all over it, mix well and serve it well chilled.

WOODRUFF 'WINE' CUP

1 pt. white wine	Orange
2 pts. red wine	Bunches of woodruff
Sugar	

Put the red and white wine into a jug with enough sugar to sweeten it. Cut the orange into thick slices and add it to the wine. Add some bunches of well-washed and dried woodruff, and leave it to infuse for 24 hours. Remove the woodruff before serving.

CHAPTER FOUR

Mixed Herb Recipes

Throughout this book there are recipes which use more than one herb, and they have been included under the heading of the main herb used; but there are some recipes which use a number of herbs mixed together, and for the convenience of the user, these are given below. There is also a certain amount of cross-referencing under the separate headings to help you to find recipes for the different herbs where more than one has been recommended. Use also the plant index.

HERB BUTTER

Butter	Dill
Mayonnaise	Dandelion leaves
Parsley	Watercress
1 Green pepper	Paprika
Green shallot tops	Thyme
Garlic	Salt and Pepper
Tarragon	

Put equivalent amounts of all the vegetables through a blender, add the salt, pepper, paprika, garlic, thyme and tarragon, and blend them well into soft butter with a little mayonnaise added. Spread this on biscuits or bread.

CHIVRY BUTTER AND SAUCE RAVIGOTE

1 dspn. each of:	Burnet
parsley	chives
tarragon	2 tbsp. shallots
chervil	¾ lb. butter

Blanch the herbs for 3 minutes in salted water. Chop the shallots and blanch them separately. Drain the herbs and dip them in cold water and dry them with a clean cloth. Pound them in a mortar or a blender with the shallots and add the butter. When the whole lot is blended together, rub it through a fine sieve.

To make Sauce Ravigote, add some of this butter to ordinary white sauce, plus a little white wine, a squirt of lemon juice, a touch of garlic and a pinch of mustard.

HERB MAYONNAISE

Mayonnaise

2 tbsp. fresh herbs
  (chervil, tarragon, watercress, chives, etc., etc.)

Use the mayonnaise recipe (see below) with 2 tablespoons of fresh herbs well blended in.

Mayonnaise: 1–2 egg yolks, ¼ pt. salad oil, salt, 1 tspn. vinegar or lemon juice. Add some oil, drop by drop into the whisked egg yolks, whisking both all the time. Add the vinegar or lemon juice and salt, whisk again, and then slowly add and whisk in the rest of the oil.

FRESH HERB AND CREAM DRESSING

½ pt. sour cream or yoghurt

2–3 tbsp. chopped mixed herbs

2 hard boiled eggs

Juice of half a lemon

Sugar

Salt

Mix the cream or yoghurt with the lemon juice, stir in the chopped eggs and herbs and season with sugar and salt to taste. This dressing is excellent with boiled beef.

FRESH SPRING HERB SOUP

2 tbsp. chopped herbs
  (dandelion, nettle, sorrel, milfoil, ground ivy and chervil)

1½ oz. butter

1½ oz. flour

2¼ pts. stock

1 egg yolk

Salt

Wash and chop the herbs and fry them in the hot fat. Add

the flour, stirring carefully for a couple of minutes. Add the stock gradually, and bring it to the boil. Simmer for 5 minutes, season and add the egg yolk beaten in a little water.

HERB BREAD

1 French loaf   1 tbsp. mixed herbs
2½ oz. butter

The herbs for this recipe can be varied according to taste. Parsley, chives, rosemary, lemon thyme; or parsley, chives and fennel for serving with fish; or parsley, chives, marjoram, thyme and chervil. Mix the herbs into the softened butter. Cut the loaf into diagonal slices ½ in. thick, but not right through. Spread each slice with some of the butter, press the loaf together again and then wrap it in foil. Cook it in a hot oven for about 15 minutes.

HERBED EGGS IN ROLLS

Fresh herbs (chives,   Cheese spread, or grated
   marjoram, mint, fennel,   cheese
   garlic, horseradish,   Eggs
   savory, chervil or basil)   Butter
Round bread rolls   Salt and pepper

Cut the rolls in half and scoop out the soft bread inside them. For each half roll use 1 oz. of cheese spread with one or two of the chopped herbs, with salt and pepper rubbed well in. Line the roll with this mixture and break an egg in each, with a spot of butter on top of that. Bake them in a moderate oven for about 15 minutes, or until the eggs are just set, but not hard.

HOT SAUCE

¼ lb. garlic   1 small bottle soy
1 tspn. celery seeds   sauce
1 stick cinnamon   Vinegar
¼ lb. mixed spice   Walnut pickle vinegar
¼ lb. horseradish   Onion pickle vinegar

Put the garlic and horseradish through a mincer. Boil all the spices in vinegar and when they are cold, mix them with the garlic, horseradish and celery seeds. Pour them into a large Kilner jar with some walnut vinegar, onion pickle vinegar and the soy. Shake the jar frequently.

GREEN DUMPLINGS

Make ordinary dumplings with suet and flour, seasoned with salt and pepper. Pick green buds of hawthorn, tips of nettles, grass, dandelion leaves, daisy stems, shoots of young corn, turnip tops and other herbs and wild plants mentioned in this book. Wash and chop them finely. Work the herbs into the dough until it is quite green. These dumplings are excellent in stews or soup.

OXYGARUM AND OLEOGARUM

The Gauls loved spiced dishes, and here are two which could be experimented with. (Note: a scruple is 1/24 of an ounce).

Oxygarum sauce for boiled or roast game: $\frac{1}{2}$ oz. pepper, 3 scruples of masterwort, 6 scruples of cardomom grains, 6 scruples of dried mint leaves, 6 scruples of dried mint flowers. Mix these after grinding them very finely with honey, and just before serving add a little broth or vinegar.

Oleogarum, to be served with fried snails: Lovage, coriander, rue, broth, honey and a little oil. Or thyme, savory, pepper, honey, broth and oil.

MIXED HERB DRINK RECIPES

HERB WINE

Mint	Basil, etc., etc.
Thyme	Water
Sage	Sugar
Agrimony	$\frac{1}{2}$ tspn. yeast
Marjoram	

Soak the herbs in water. Allow 3 lb. sugar to each gallon of water. Boil the herbs with the sugar and water they have soaked in until all the flavour is extracted. Strain the juice into a fermentation jar when it is cool, and add $\frac{1}{2}$ teaspoonful of yeast. Mature, rack and bottle in the usual way.

METHEGLIN

4 lb. honey	2 cloves
1 gal. water	$\frac{1}{4}$ oz. cinnamon bark, or
Juice of 2 lemons	Caraway seeds
$\frac{1}{2}$ oz. yeast	Marjoram
1 tspn. nutrient	Balm
1 oz. hops	Mace
$\frac{1}{2}$ oz. root ginger	Strawberry leaves, etc.

Metheglin is mead with herbs and spices added and the permutations are endless. It depends on what you like best. Simmer the herbs and spices in water for $\frac{1}{2}$ hour then strain them on to the honey. Boil the liquid for another 2 hours, skimming all the time. When cool add the nutrient, lemon juice and yeast and put it into a fermentation jar. Finish as usual.

WHITE METHEGLIN (Old recipe)

'Take of Sweet-briar a great handful; of Violet flowers, Sweet-marjoram, Strawberry leaves, Violet leaves, and one handful Agrimony, Bugloss, Borrage, and half a handful of Rosemary; four branches Gilliflowers (the yellow wallflowers with great tops), anniseeds, Fennel and Caraway, of each a spoonful, two large Mace. Boil all these in twelve gallons of water for the space of an hour; then strain it, and let it stand until it be Milk-warm. Then put in as much honey as will carry an Egge to the breadth of sixpence at least, then boil it again, and scum it clean; then let stand, until it be cold, then put a pint of Ale-barm into it, and ripen it as you do Beer, and tun it. Then hang in the midst of the vessel a little bag with a Nutmeg quartered, a Race of Ginger sliced, a little Cinnamon, and Mace whole, and three grains of Musk in a cloth put into the bag amongst the rest of the Spices. Put a stone in the bag, to keep it amongst the rest of the Liquour. This quantity took up three gallons of honey; therefore be sure to have four in readiness.'

HIGHLAND BITTERS

1¾ oz. gentian root
½ oz. Seville orange peel
1 cinnamon stick
1 oz. coriander seed

¼ oz. chamomile flowers
½ oz. whole cloves
2 bottles whisky

Chop finely the gentian root and the orange peel. Add the coriander seed, chamomile flowers, cinnamon and cloves. Pound all these well, then put them into earthenware or Kilner jars, pour the whisky over, seal the jars firmly and leave them for 10 days. Strain and bottle. The flavouring materials may be used more than once, just pour more whisky over them.

A similar drink can be made with chamomile flowers, bitter orange peel and juniper berries.

VESPETRO

3 oz. angelica seed
½ oz. aniseed
½ oz. fennel seed
2 oz. coriander seed
Brandy

Strong syrup (see
    page 25)
6 oz. sliced orange
6 oz. sliced lemon

Put the seeds and fruits into a Kilner jar and top up with brandy. Steep for a month, shaking the bottle from time to time. Strain the liqueur and add it to about half as much strong syrup.

This drink is good for the digestion.

AQUA VITAE COMPOSITAE (A sixteenth-century recipe)

'Take one gallon of strong French wine, and of sage, mints, red roses, thyme, pellitory, rosemary, wild thyme, chamomile, lavendar each a handful. These herbs shall be stamped all together in a mortar and then put in a clean vessel with a pint of rosewater and a quart of Spanish wine, and closely stoppered and let to stand so three or four days. Then put into a still and distil it once. Then take your distilled water and pour it back again upon the herbs in the still, and strew upon it these powders following; cloves and cinnamon, of each half an ounce, orris, one ounce, a few maces, nutmegs half an ounce, a little saffron, musk, spikenard, amber; and put some camphor in it. Stir all well together, and distil it clean off, till it come fat like oil, then get away the distilled water and let it be well kept (in bottles). After that make a strong fire and distil oil of what is left, and receive it in a phial. (It is wonderful good!)'

'CHARTREUSE'

1 lb. 7 oz. balm

11 oz. angelica leaves

1 lb. 8 oz. hyssop

$3\frac{1}{2}$ oz. cinnamon

$1\frac{1}{2}$ oz. saffron

$1\frac{1}{2}$ oz. mace

$2\frac{1}{2}$ lb. sugar

11 qts. distilled alcohol

Infuse all these together for 10 days. Perhaps this is the recipe used by the monks of Chartreux!

Plant Index

Recipes Index

CONFECTIONS, CAKES AND BISCUITS

DESSERTS

215

DRINKS

FISH DISHES

FLAVOURINGS

MEAT, POULTRY AND GAME DISHES

PRESERVES AND JAMS

PICKLES AND CHUTNEYS

SOUPS

SUPPER DISHES, SNACKS AND ENTREES

VEGETABLES